Diary of an Awakening
A Spiritual Journey Of A Lifetime

Jenice Meagher Cutler

Inner Avenue Media

Inner Avenue Media
P.O. Box 271654
Fort Collins, CO 80527
www.inneravenue.com

© Copyright 2002. Jenice Meagher Cutler.
All Rights Reserved

No part of this book may be reproduced or copied in any form or by any means—graphic, electronic or mechanical—without the written permission of the publisher except in the case of brief quotations embodied in critical articles and reviews.

The author gratefully acknowledges permissions from these sources to reprint the following:

Portions from *Opening to Channel: How to Connect with Your Guide* by Sanaya Roman and Duane Packer, H J Kramer Inc., 1987.

An excerpt from *Conversations with God: an uncommon dialogue (Book 1)* by Neale Donald Walsch, G. P. Putnam's Sons, 1996 (originally published by Hampton Roads Publishing Company, Inc., 1995).

An excerpt from *Conversations with God: an uncommon dialogue (Book 2)* by Neale Donald Walsch, Hampton Roads Publishing Company, Inc., 1997.

Cover Design by Foster & Foster, Inc.
Interior Design & Typesetting by Desktop Miracles, Inc.

ISBN 0-9712133-0-5

Printed in the United States of America

Dedication

*To Trey, my partner for spiritual growth,
Who lives life from the inside out; illuminates love,
integrity, compassion; rejoices in the journey; sees no
barriers; and creates Heaven on earth.*

*For God,
This is yours. I am yours.*

Acknowledgments

My love and gratitude to my three children through whom I have learned the great lesson that no one and nothing is mine, that when I release and set free, my love grows deeper, healthier, purer.

Thank you to Jill Mason for your insightful editorial suggestions.

My deep appreciation to my soulfriends, Laura Hajovsky, Jennifer Mosle, and Lauren King, for giving me the opportunity to share my spiritual experience with you shortly after it happened (I remember how and where I told each of you) and for your overwhelming and unwavering acceptance and support; for reading numerous drafts of this book over the five years it took to write; for sharing your journeys with me, helping me to broaden and grow; and for generously sharing your beauty and love.

I also thank Sharla Myers for your friendship, which played an integral role in my spiritual opening and awakening.

I thank Father George Yandell whose matter of fact acceptance of my experience encouraged me along my journey instead of halting me with doubts and fear.

My eternal gratitude to Erin Kramp for opening my eyes and heart to the depths with which I could experience God, for being the catalyst to the beauty that my life has become.

And finally, Trey, words cannot express the magnitude of my love and gratitude, and yet, you know. I have experienced the oneness of spirit, life, and love, as our spirits have merged with each other and with God.

Contents

PART I
My Spiritual Experience

INTRODUCTION	In Preparation for the Journey	1
CHAPTER ONE	Day One: Affirmation of Spiritual Connection	16
CHAPTER TWO	Day Two: Drawn to My Guide	22
CHAPTER THREE	Day Three: The Path to Channeling	25
CHAPTER FOUR	Day Four: The Hands	28
CHAPTER FIVE	Day Five: Contact!	34
CHAPTER SIX	Day Six: Birth and Blossoming	45
CHAPTER SEVEN	Day Seven: Revelations	77

PART II
Lessons Learned

CHAPTER EIGHT	The Gift of Time and Experience	89
CHAPTER NINE	Perspective Now	93
CHAPTER TEN	Love	109
CHAPTER ELEVEN	Honesty	118
CHAPTER TWELVE	Clearing and Cleansing	127
CHAPTER THIRTEEN	Creating False Realities	138
CHAPTER FOURTEEN	Free Will and the Game of Life	142

Chapter Fifteen	Spirituality and Religion	146
Chapter Sixteen	Looking Closer at Ourselves	167
Chapter Seventeen	Evil and Death	181
Chapter Eighteen	Living an Awakened Life	198
Appendix A	Trey's Perspective	208
Appendix B	Channeling	217
Closing Thoughts		227

PART I

My Spiritual Experience

INTRODUCTION

In Preparation for the Journey

WHAT WOULD YOU DO IF YOUR LIFE was forever changed by a dramatic and bizarre sequence of spiritual experiences that unfolded in one week? How would you be different if you were suddenly able to access spirits beyond this world? How would you respond to a face-to-face encounter with Jesus? What new direction would your life take? What would you value most? This is what my story is about.

I am the neighbor down the street or the lady you're always running into at the grocery, no more or less remarkable than the people you encounter on a daily basis. Yet the experience I had and will share with you is remarkable. I will set it before you with honesty, which is painfully embarrassing at times, and with my own amazement that this incredible experience happened to me.

Over a mere seven days, I hiked a magnificent mountain and reached a summit few people experience in life. For a brief time after this journey, I was allowed to remain at the top, the crisp, clear skies enabling me to see what I am usually unable to see. And then I slowly descended, not retracing my tracks, but rather down the other side, to a new place, better equipped than before to continue my journey of life.

I feel after talking with two priests at my Episcopal church, as well as with others familiar with spiritual experiences, that my encounter with the Divine is unique in many ways and yet possesses threads of familiarity and commonality linking it to the experiences of others. My experience was an eye-opener for me, and I feel that it has the potential to open willing eyes everywhere. Those of you who are deep into the mystical, spiritual nature of our existence will see the beauty and truth in my experience, which will support and supplement your existing knowledge. Those who are searching for an affirmation of the existence of God and the afterlife or for the purpose in life can discover the truth through my story. There is in fact a spiritual realm beyond our earthly, physical plane that is continuously with us and helping us on our spiritual paths. I long to help others to cross the bridge from ambivalence to faith, or from faith to knowledge.

I believe God gave me this experience as much for others as for myself. For several years prior to this experience, I was at a wonderful place in life, neither needing nor seeking a mountaintop experience. I was truly happy, secure and aware of God's presence and blessings in my life. I wasn't searching for anything, there was no crisis in my life, and, as far as I knew, I didn't need anything. My life was as perfect as I think life can be before a Divine encounter. And then, in effect, God broadsided me with this gift. He was telling me that it was time to wake up and open my eyes to His workings, so that I could grow with Him and then share this knowledge with others.

Although I know my experience was meant to be shared, I also know that it will engender a wide range of reactions. On the negative side, some people will think I'm crazy, some will think I'm a liar, some will think I created this out of some hidden need, and the list goes on. I have to admit that the anticipated negative opinions rattle my security and courage a little, yet I expect them and I know that I must respect them, as each of us is at a different stage in our spiritual journeys. Even my parents and siblings wonder why I don't keep this personal experience personal, seeing no value in "fixing" my life when it isn't broken. Three reasons come to mind. First, Jesus Himself told me that my purpose at this time is to share His gift to me with others. I gave Jesus my will, He let His desire for me be known, and I'm fulfilling His wish despite having some of my own reservations. Second, after sharing my experience with family and friends, I have witnessed the potential it has to open the hearts of others, empowering them to recognize their own spiritual essence and connection to God. Of course, that is the purpose of sharing the experience, and, selfishly, when others are inspired to tap into their own spirituality, the foundation of my own security and courage is strengthened. Third, I now possess a broader understanding of God and a profound sense of peace in that understanding. I wish for all others who are seeking a deeper relationship with God to share in my knowledge and God's peace.

Packing The Baggage

I did not always possess the peace that I now enjoy. For the first ten years of life, I grew up in a dysfunctional home. My biological father was a violent alcoholic, a wife batterer, and an adulterer. My mother bore the brunt of his physical abuse, but we all suffered tremendously from his emotional abuse. I know my mother did her best to protect us from him, but as the oldest of three children, I was aware of, and suffered greatly from, this man's destructive nature. As a child, I did not know that my family was different from others, nor did I grasp the extent of my scarring.

While I don't think that my father is purely bad, nor was all the time with him bad, the moments that leave the most lasting impressions on a young child are the negative ones, the moments of fear and confusion and pain. For me those moments included being frequently awakened in the middle of the night by my parents' screaming and yelling and then trying to comfort and protect my scared and crying younger brother; never knowing what would trigger my father's rage but frequently setting him off and feeling that it was always my fault and that something was wrong with me; being black and blue from belt whippings; getting thrown out of restaurants because of my dad's drunken scenes (this was extremely embarrassing and made every outing tense because I never was certain whether he would behave or not); enduring my father's guilt trips and twisted emotional manipulation—it was the kids' fault for his lack of attention and love; fearing for my life when he was driving drunk and jumping curbs and running red lights; spending the night at a neighbor's, hearing sirens, and looking out the window to see the police taking my dad; hearing my father threaten to throw acid in my mom's face so that no other man would want her and to kill the man who would become my stepfather . . . these are just a few frames from a long and dark picture.

One particular image from my childhood is seared in my mind, never to be forgotten. I guess I was around six or seven years old when I was awakened in the middle of the night by my mother's frantic screaming. She was calling my name over and over. I followed her calls down the hall and into the kitchen. The visual image that remains with me is of my mother draped across the floor, up on one elbow, with blood and tears on her face and intense fear and desperation in her eyes. My father stood above her, drunk and angry. The emotional image that remains with me is my complete sense of helplessness and confusion. Mom was begging me, pleading with me, to go get our neighbors, to please get someone to help. My father was threatening me not to move, not to take a step. I was completely torn; I wanted to help my mom more than anything, but I was scared to death of my dad. The fear and conflict that I felt literally paralyzed me. I could neither move nor think.

And then I lost it. I remember crying hysterically in the kitchen and then "coming to" with my father sitting on my bed telling me everything was going to be okay. It was as if my mind short-circuited for a brief time because of my inability to deal with the situation.

I do not fault my mom for the emotional baggage I carried inside as a child, adolescent, and young adult, which I successfully hid from most people. She grew up in a dysfunctional home and then married young, before having worked through her own issues. She did the best she was able to do. When I was eleven, she married a man who had custody of his four children. She was two days short of her thirty-second birthday when she became a mother of seven. Because of her own problems and pain while married to my father, and then the impossibility of focusing on any one child when you have seven, my mother did not provide that one strong, unconditionally loving influence in my life that I needed to build my sense of security and self-worth. Of course, she loved me as only a parent can; she saved me from my dad, who was the single most destructive influence on my life; and she also provided a "normal" home for seven young children from two torn households.

Unpacking The Baggage

When my mom became engaged to my stepfather, I begged her not to marry him, although I didn't share with her my reason. I saw her marriage as another rejection of my love. I had lost my father, and now I was losing my mother, to a man I did not know well. All of their friends advised against marriage as well, predicting failure. Thankfully, my parents did not heed our advice, although it did take many trying and difficult years to reach the "Brady Bunch" level of harmony. Bolstered by love and time, these two dysfunctional, damaged families merged into one functional, loving family. My stepfather is my father in every respect except blood, and when I refer to my "dad" now, I'm referring to him. My dad was the first gift that I recognized as being from God, although this awareness came later in life. His strength, goodness, and love, all stemming from his strong religious convictions, bonded our families and gave us all a chance at life.

Most of us who have grown up with dysfunction must confront that dysfunction at some point in our lives in order to move on and heal. In a sense, my life has been a continuous climb from this oftentimes desperate and painful childhood to higher, happier, and more peaceful grounds. But this climb was not without help. Initially, I sought my identity in good grades and popularity contests; they were my first building blocks to security and self-worth. When I was seventeen years old, God sent me a boyfriend, John, whom I consider my savior. He was in my life until my mid-twenties. He saw goodness in me that I couldn't see. He saw worthiness in me that I couldn't feel. He helped me remove the sins of my biological father from myself. John was the answer to my recurrent prayer: "Help me to know that I can love others and that I can be loved by others." He truly was a gift from God. And he loved me so unconditionally and counseled me so well that I am able to be a happy, emotionally healthy, secure, and worthy person today.

I hardly recall the Jenice I was in my youth. I am so far removed from her that it is as if she is another person with another life. She seems to be distinct from me and the pain she bore is largely gone, although rationally I know she is my root and foundation. In other words, I do not dwell upon the dysfunction in my past. But I also acknowledge that we all must deal with the challenges in our lives and that we must never forget or discredit them, because they are our mold.

I believe we have varied tools within our grasp to help us step out of the dysfunction. Those tools ultimately reside within us, even when we seek external assistance. I was fortunate for having intelligence, strength, a yearning for something better, and compassionate people entering my life. Yet there remains an unfairness I do not understand. Why was I fortunate enough to break the cycle of dysfunction when so many are not?

Even Lighter Load

Because of my childhood and for as far back as I can remember, my first priority and only dream in life was to have that normal, functional, loving family that I saw glimpses of through friends and neighbors. I had always believed that to realize that dream, I must place my primary focus on my kids and on being the best mother possible. However, through premarital counseling required by our church, I learned that I must focus on my role as spouse first: through a healthy, attentive, and loving relationship with my husband, our children would learn and gain the most. This transition in focus did not come easily for me, which brings me to where I was when this journey began.

I was thirty-five years old and married almost seven years with two children: a four-and-a-half-year-old girl and a boy just turning three years old. My husband, Trey, was a partner at a large Dallas law firm. We had met and started dating in law school and married four years later. I practiced business law for five years and then quit to stay at home when our daughter was born. I loved being a mom, and our kids were the center of my life. We lived a middle- to upper middle-class lifestyle that provided our children with many opportunities. Trey was an involved, attentive father and a loving, sensitive husband. Together we had created the family that I had longed for in my youth.

We felt incredibly blessed by the love, health, and comfort in our lives. But that didn't mean that life was stress free or that I never lost my patience with the kids or got sick of the monotony of the household chores or drank too much every once in a while as a release or took out my frustrations and stress on my husband, because I did. Arguing kids, financial burdens, and time constraints presented us with struggles on a daily basis, just as they do any family. But we were very fortunate not to have any significant negatives pulling us away from happiness and growth. As you may be able to glean from this description of our life, we were fairly risk-averse, introspective, analytical people.

Equipment And Training

My relationship with God began in my early teens as a result of my leap of faith after the boy next door shared his religious faith with me. I prayed desperately for God to give me any sign of His existence, like speaking out loud or moving something in my room. But He didn't. My initial "experimental" commitment to God was founded on my great need for love and for the existence of a meaningful purpose in life, rather than on any sense of God's existence or presence in my life. When you see nothing or no one to turn to, especially as a teen with few resources for counseling and love, it makes sense to give religion a try. And maybe this sincere attempt at religion during my teens, as I became aware of my life's circumstances and that I had some control over them, is what set me on the path of function over dysfunction. Over time, my faith transcended need and evolved into a real relationship with God. It is ironic that the manifest sign of God's existence that I so desperately prayed for in my teens came twenty years later when I had a strong faith and no longer needed the sign.

Through the years my focus on God has ebbed and flowed. Generally, I've prayed on a somewhat regular basis, although I've attended church irregularly. I grew up Catholic and converted to Episcopalian when Trey and I married. We became more involved with our Episcopal church after the kids were born. At the time of my experience, I was finishing up my first year of teaching both Vacation Bible School and Sunday School. I assume these are common experiences for many people, that is, commitment as convenient. I never considered giving my will to God, as that was something the truly devoted religious folks did. I had never attempted to read the Bible, although I read to my children from children's or beginner's Bibles. And of course, I am familiar with excerpts from the Bible through attending church and Sunday School. Because I didn't preach God and religion to others, and because I'm fun-loving and innocuously rebellious at times, many acquaintances probably had no idea that I was religious. But I did have a relationship with God that I just kept to myself. That relationship was personal and close, rather than academic and distant. It was real. At times, I felt God's presence in my life.

Perhaps the snapshot of my religious state of mind at the time can best be summarized by the prayer I said night after night:

> Dear God: Thank you for all the blessings in my life, especially for my two kids and my wonderful husband. Thank you for the kids' health, goodness, intelligence, and cuteness, and I pray that they may have long, happy, and healthy lives. Please help me to do all that I can to help that occur for them. Please help me to be the best mom and wife that I can be. I pray for . . . [specific needs of family and friends]. Please help me to be aware of others' needs so that I can help them and please help others through me. Also, help me to listen to you with an open heart. Thank you for leading me to screenwriting, and I selfishly pray that I will be successful at it someday. Forgive me for all my sins. Please help us to know whether or not to have more children [recent addition]. Amen.

I could honestly say that I knew God had answered many prayers over the course of my life. At first I realized this in hindsight, but within the past few years, I had begun to recognize God's answers as they unfolded. I was learning how to "listen" to God. One of God's answers came after I quit work to stay at home with our children. I was regularly praying to know what to do with the rest of my life. I would not practice law again, as it was a struggle and stress for me on a daily basis. But what would I do? God led me to screenwriting. Believe me, I had to be paying attention to His signs to get there. Technical writing and analytical thinking had been my focus for years, and I didn't write poetry, short stories, or any other form of creative writing. I recognized God's guiding me to writing through subtle influences that aroused my attention and interest, like new relationships with writers and encouraging responses from family and friends to whom I had merely written cards, leading me to discover a passion that I never knew I had.

My intent in mentioning screenwriting, especially considering I've written only two movies, neither of which has sold, is simply to share with you that with my discovery of screenwriting came a time of wonderful transition in my life; I opened new doors that enabled my life to grow and expand. For the first time, I had a personal dream that extended beyond the functionality of my family. The possibility of selling a movie spawned an invigoration and excitement in me that I had never felt before. I realized how I had fallen asleep in life, becoming comfortable with the cobwebs of limitation that I was spinning. In recognizing how I had capped my own potential, I saw how many of us seem more comfortable in complacency, preferring to shelter rather than challenge and expand ourselves.

Self-Drawn Map

Before the experience described later in this book, I believed Jesus to be the son of God, although my focus was mainly on God. I felt that Jesus was one, but not the only, way to Heaven. I admitted to not being a "true Christian" in that respect. To me, the key was the pursuit of goodness. I could never get past the fact that most of us are of a particular faith or religion because of the home we're born into. Accordingly, I could not accept that the luck of the draw dictated whether one is entitled to God's salvation. I assume most if not all religions believe their way is the right way. So if exclusivity holds true, don't you hope you were born in the right home in the right part of the world? It just couldn't work that way. How could any of us assume that our human-made interpretations and rules are the sole correct way? How could a good person, regardless of his or her religious affiliation or lack thereof, not go to Heaven? Interestingly, my religious beliefs haven't changed dramatically since the experience, although they have evolved in a sense.

Uncharted Territory

I have always had a fun and casual curiosity about spiritual, metaphysical, and mystical philosophies, as well as an openness to their ideas. When I was in college in my early twenties, my mom arranged for my astrological charting. This was entertaining and memorable on two counts: first, I was told that the second half of my life would be immensely happy, far exceeding the first half of life; and second, I was advised to take a creative writing class. Both of these messages stuck with me because, at the time, they seemed unlikely.

With respect to the first, I was at a place in life where I thought the purpose of life was solely for being tested. God would throw bad stuff at us intermittently throughout our life, and we passed the test if we still had faith and were good people. Life sure wasn't about happiness, but wouldn't it be great if it was? As far as writing, I didn't have the slightest inclination or aptitude, although a few years later, I would enhance my writing skills in law school and through practicing law. This was the only recommendation of the reader that I felt was totally off the mark with respect to who and where I was. Funny though, I never forgot it, and it came to fruition ten years later, partly for that reason.

I had talked with two psychics, both in the year immediately prior to my experience, and both at events where the psychic was "free entertainment." I had read two spiritual books: *Celestine Prophecy* by James Redfield and *Embraced by the Light* by Betty J. Eadie. I feel that both books served as a catalyst for my experience. I generally believed *Embraced by the Light*, although I didn't dwell on it. It broadened my view of how God's kingdom might work. For example, it had never occurred to me that our spirits might exist before life on earth. I became more open-minded and less structured in my thinking because of Eadie's experience. After reading *Celestine Prophecy*, I felt connected to the spiritual realm for the first time. This connection seemed to last for a few weeks and then was gone. What I mean by spiritually connected is that I felt energized, I recognized a few "coincidences" in my life, which the book emphasized that we should pay attention to, and many of the book's insights rang true with me. Not a big deal, but just new and exciting feelings.

I hope that you can tell from this information that my spiritual experience did not result from a lifelong interest in the metaphysical. That's not to say that I wasn't interested in the spiritual, as two of my favorite movies are *It's a Wonderful Life* and *Heaven Can Wait* and the first movie I wrote was spiritual. But I was like a lot of people: I had my traditional religious relationship with God; I primarily focused on earthly matters; I tried to lead a good life, hoping to make the cut into Heaven; and I tried to be nonjudgmental and open-minded in general. Spirituality fell into a category not too different from that of homosexuality, in that I was much more comfortable with and accepting of the concept as long as it happened to someone else. Furthermore, just as I believed in God, Jesus, and angels, I also believed in an evil force or being. I feared that if I opened myself up more directly to the good, then I automatically opened myself up to the bad as well. That theory was too scary and intimidating to test. Some distance provided comfort.

Two Guides

One person's death and another person's continuing battle with death have taken me down paths that I wouldn't have traveled on my own. I was twenty-nine years old when my brother Craig died at the age of twenty-six in October of 1990. Now I am a member of a "club" that I didn't know existed and had no facility to understand until his death. The bond of this club is the loss of a loved one. I believe most of us can understand such pain and loss only by living through it.

In Preparation for the Journey

Although I wish Craig hadn't died prematurely, I am an immensely better person because of his death, as it spawned growth that would have been inaccessible to me without such tragedy. Of the many facets to this experience and the resulting growth, two changes in my perspective have dramatically affected my life: 1) I now see life as unpredictable and potentially short, which helps me to appreciate the need to make the most of each and every day, and 2) because I understand death, loss, and pain through every cell of my being, I have gained a deeper level of compassion and am no longer uncomfortable expressing my compassion in difficult circumstances.

Before Craig's death, when I encountered others who had recently lost a loved one, I would avoid them in order to avoid confronting their loss; I didn't know the right thing to say and I didn't want to upset them. Although I hurt for those people and prayed for them, I didn't have any experience to help me understand or deal with their grief. Now I know that there are no "right" things to say or magical words that will take away the pain but that *showing* compassion through caring words and actions does provide comfort and support to survivors. We can acknowledge their pain, let them know that we care for them, that we're hurting for them, that we're praying for them, and that we're there for them if they need us. Grieving means experiencing all of the emotions that arise upon a great loss, so by offering an opportunity to talk and a shoulder to cry on, we open the door for their expression of grief. There is beauty and healing in the gift of an open door, whether the survivor chooses to walk through it or not, for it is a gift of love and compassion. I personally wanted to talk about Craig's death, as there was little else on my mind. I had to work through it, understand it, and assimilate the reality of it. I was immensely grateful to those friends who were willing to share in my pain.

Something happened to me at the time of Craig's death that significantly impacted my husband's view of the world in two ways: he saw what happened to me as a sign of an inherent spiritual link among us humans, and as a sign of some unseen force at work in our lives. My brother had developed epilepsy when he was eighteen, and for a significant time before his death, he was having seizures frequently. On the night he died, Trey and I were in our bedroom watching TV. Out of nowhere, I felt as if I was going to be sick. I went into the bathroom and, for about five minutes, had violent dry heaves. Then, just as suddenly as the spell had begun, it was over, and I was fine. About thirty minutes later, Craig's wife phoned us with the brief message that Craig was at the hospital and that we needed to come immediately. When we arrived, we learned that he was dead. He had died during a seizure by asphyxiating on his vomit—at the same time I had the dry heaves.

My comfort with addressing painful situations explains why Erin Kramp, now dealing with death on a daily basis, has become such a significant influence in my life. Erin and Trey became close friends in junior high and high school. She and her husband, Doug, were people we liked a lot but saw infrequently, due to our similarly busy schedules. In January of 1994, one month shy of her thirty-second birthday, Erin was diagnosed with breast cancer. Her daughter was twenty-two months old. Because of Craig's death and having two young children of my own, I couldn't keep myself from standing in her shoes. The thought of Erin leaving her daughter motherless was unbearable to me. I was drawn to her. I wanted to help in any way I could. I feel that our friendship was strengthened largely because of my willingness to talk with her about the reality of her situation.

At the time of my experience, Erin was finishing up eleven months of treatment on her second round of breast cancer, which had spread to her spine. Erin is the most spiritually connected person I know, and I thank her with my whole heart for forthrightly sharing her "connectedness" with me. Although she had had Divine encounters throughout her life, those encounters had dramatically increased in frequency since the onset of her cancer. Her willingness to share her experiences helped me to accept the spiritual world's interaction with humanity, even though I had not directly experienced anything similar myself.

To My Fellow Travelers

I admit that when I was given this experience, I questioned why I was chosen when there are so many people more committed and devoted to God than I. I do not have an answer. Since God is for the most part invisible to us, something we feel and experience within ourselves, I can no more convince anyone of God's existence than I can convince anyone that this experience really happened to me. But it is not my purpose to persuade anyone of the legitimacy of my experience, or to convert them to my beliefs. My story will be powerful for some and reach them now, for others it will be a seed for later growth, and for others still it will serve as no more than conversational or gossip value. I am at peace with any and all responses because my purpose is simply to present my experience and what I have learned and then to allow God to work through it for others in accordance with His plan. So I present the story of my amazing week to you the best I can, as a mother and wife, a daughter and sister, a friend and stranger, but mostly as a child of God and, therefore, as your sister in God's kingdom.

ONE

Affirmation of Spiritual Connection

day one

Sunday evening, May 5, 1996

CLOSE FRIENDS HAD INVITED OUR FAMILY to attend a fundraiser at the Dallas Zoo for a charitable organization that helps children with AIDS. The sky was blue, the entertainment abundant, and the food and beer free with admission, making for a very enjoyable evening. After having their faces painted and playing with the clowns, the kids participated in a concert by a great local entertainer. I took the opportunity to visit with the free psychic while Trey watched the kids.

The psychic asked whether I had a specific question or just wanted to know generally about the next year. I hesitated, unsure myself, and then decided on a particular question that I had frequently pondered of late: Would I be successful at screenwriting? I would later realize that, despite my having asked a specific question, she proceeded with the upcoming year's predictions. My mindset, however, was focused on screenwriting because I had asked her about it and because I was very excited about a new idea I had for a movie.

A small cloth sack with a drawstring lay on the table, and she asked me to pull out three stones. With my hand still in the bag, she asked if I was pregnant. I wasn't, and I told her so. (I was thinking that she was able to read my mind because I had a strong drive to have a third child. Trey and I were confronting the issue but were feeling that rational considerations indicated that we shouldn't.) Then I pulled out the mother and child stones, which she said meant that I would have a baby within the next year. I was interested yet apprehensive. Trey and I had promised Erin that upon her death we would become a second family to her daughter, and I didn't want this addition to our family to be because of Erin's passing. Without addressing the third rock, the psychic asked me to draw three more rocks. Those rocks were negative, courage, and wisdom.

As the psychic spoke, I was very focused on her face, often staring intently into her eyes. At some point, I became aware of a magnificent pink sunset behind her that pervaded the whole sky within my view. I shifted my focus from the psychic to the sky to take in the sunset, but the sky was blue. Looking back at her, a beautiful pink sky—back to the sky, no setting of the sun, just blueness. In my confusion, I couldn't keep from sharing with her that I was seeing a lot of pink. I literally just blurted it out. She responded that I was seeing her aura, which tends to be strong when she's working. No kidding! This was no little glow around her head. It was a sunset! I was dumbfounded, amazed, and tickled that possibly I had seen an aura. She confirmed that I had a gift I should work on and advised me not to get frustrated if I didn't see another aura for a while, as hers is stronger than most. After my acknowledgment of seeing pink, her messages became more spiritual in nature, I assume because she then thought that I would be more open to them or better understand them.

But seeing the aura didn't convince me that the psychic's words were pertinent or credible. Instead, I had fun letting my imagination explore the possibilities, for this was play, not real life, and not much different from reading the message of a fortune cookie at a Chinese restaurant. Although I did not accept her messages as my reality, I respected her and her craft, and I listened with an open and curious mind.

The psychic's messages for me (with my casual thoughts):

- I would have a baby within the year.
  (I knew we wouldn't be trying to get pregnant, if at all, within the next three months, and we know how long babies take, although conception within a year was possible.)

- I had a talent for conveying life's lessons and my movies needed to include messages about these lessons.
  (Since screenwriting was God-sent, it seemed natural that any movies I wrote should possess God's, or good, messages.)

- I would write books that would teach through pictures as well as words.
  (But that's not screenwriting!#@#!—although when I write, I do create images, so maybe that was what she was referring to, because I sure didn't want to write a book.)

- I would write great things.
  (Academy Awards, here I come.)

- Drawing the negative rock meant that negatives were leaving me. When I stated that I felt I didn't have many negatives, she said that maybe they were blocks to success.
  (Obviously, from my childhood, I had many negatives in my life, but I felt that I had been successful in eliminating most of them. Additionally, Craig's death and the birth of our children had prompted Trey and me to reflect upon the purpose of our lives and of life itself. We had discovered what truly mattered the most to us in life: leading good, caring lives as well as

Affirmation of Spiritual Connection

eliminating the negatives of life such as materialism, ego, jealousy, pessimism . . . .)

- In the following year doors would open for me because of the negatives leaving me, and it would entail my making a decision that would require courage and wisdom. Making that decision would establish me.

  (I guessed that the courage that I'd require was a movie idea that was controversial or maybe using an independent production company instead of a large, established company.)

- I had a spiritual gift that I needed to focus on, and I should look for an aura book by a woman doctor that details a whole spectrum of aura colors.

  (I was curious about this but didn't feel drawn to it or connected to it. I even asked the psychic about the value of this gift. She suggested that the purpose might be to understand people's moods and personalities so that I could help them. Although I remained ambivalent to the idea of developing this gift, I felt that seeing the aura was tangible evidence of my connection with the spiritual realm, which I might be able to develop in other ways.)

- I had had a new guide with me for the past three or four months to whom I should listen. When writing, I should close my eyes, talk to my guide, and listen to my inner voices. (Sometimes when writing I was amazed at how the material came from me, seemingly out of nowhere.) This guide would help my writing career. She even knew my guide's name but wouldn't tell me because I needed to learn it through my own spiritual growth. I asked if it was my brother Craig, who had died. She responded that Craig had brought my new guide to me and that Craig had been with me for a while, as had others.

  (I didn't quite know what to make of this.)

- Craig was preparing for his reincarnation the following year.
  (I had no opinion or clue as to reincarnation, neither belief nor disbelief, but I felt that anything was possible.)

- When I'm writing, everything else in my life falls into place; I'm happier and more positive.
  (How true! Our son was born in May '93 when our daughter was nineteen months old. Because of his work schedule, Trey was rarely at home for the two years after our son's birth. It was an extremely stressful time. So I took a creative writing class out of my need for an interest outside of my home and family. Writing became my outlet as well as a source of intellectual stimulation. It has since evolved into a spark of fun and passion in my life.)

- I need to listen to my inner voices and not lose my sense of humor.
  (I don't have a sense of humor, but I sure could use one.)

- In the past I have tended to jump into things and then put out the fires or run from the alligators, but in the future I'll investigate first and then pursue.
  (This portrayal was exactly the opposite of who I am, in my opinion. I have always had a blueprint for the big things in my life, leaving nothing to chance. So far I have lived my life according to plans. Impromptu, off-the-cuff decisions make me uncomfortable. I have hints of the "Type A" personality in that I use stress as a motivation and I only see what is left to do instead of appreciating how much I've done. Also, my rational nature was what was preventing us from going forward with a third child. If a third child was to be, I would have to play with fire and taunt the alligators and then trust that all would be okay. I think that in her interpretation or translation, the psychic flip-flopped this message.)

Affirmation of Spiritual Connection

⁂ I'd be sending someone to her in the next couple of months. *(Last-minute marketing.)*

She had definitely sparked my interest, and I wanted more information. I wanted to hear, "Yes, you are going to sell a movie soon." However, I sensed that she was holding back, as if she knew more but was not willing to share it with me, and then she dismissed me to the handwriting analyst.

After talking with the handwriting expert, I couldn't wait to tell Trey what had just happened. The psychic's predictions were interesting, but the aura thing, wow, that was wild, that was *me*; I saw it and couldn't deny it. Erin had often said that I had a spiritual gift that I just didn't see or acknowledge. She said we all do. Maybe she was right! Although I had never given much thought to auras, having no doubt that I had seen one this day energized me, as I saw it as a sign that I might be more spiritually connected than I realized.

When we got home, I was forced to bathe the kids despite the late hour to remove the paint and grime covering their precious little bodies. I used this time to reflect on the evening's events. Curiously, the names "Amy" and "Allison" popped into my head. I made notes of my experiences in a journal.

TWO

Drawn To My Guide

day two

Monday, May 6, 1996

A T 5:10 A.M., I AWOKE FROM A WILD DREAM. Some dreams tap deeper into our emotions and seem to be more real and significant than typical dreams. This was definitely one of those, and it left me feeling excited and a bit unsettled. I had learned in my creative writing class to write down dreams for potential material. Here is what I wrote in my "five o'clock in the morning voice," almost verbatim:

> I'm dreaming about when people die and sort of seeing the process of them leaving their bodies or saying bye (an odd dream letting me know I'm in spiritual level of sleep)—then I'm sitting on the floor of a school hall with Trey telling him about my dream and I sense, but don't see, someone walking by—a spirit—and I feel her warmth and see her footsteps and then the outline of her body/shadow as she walks toward a door with light coming in. I almost see through her. I ask Trey if he sees

her and he doesn't. She turns the corner as if she's headed for a school bathroom. She turns back around, not too much later, and walks toward me and still Trey doesn't see. She starts handing me a folder and stumbles purposely into me so that I reach out and take the folder and then her, like she tricks me to reach out. I sneeze when she enters me. I'd say she's seven-ish. I have the goose bumps as I'm writing and shivering. My guide?

Again I have the goose bumps reliving this dream, but I also have a smile.

Trey awoke from the commotion of my recording the dream on paper. He saw me shivering uncontrollably and sensed my queer state, so he held me tight as I told him my dream. As my mind wandered through the previous day's events and the dream, I questioned if the girl could be my new guide, which the psychic said Craig had sent me. Trey reacted as you might expect when a man holds his wife in the middle of the night—he wanted sex. But one of the kids had sneaked into bed with us, so he was out of luck.

At a reasonable hour of the morning, I called Erin to tell her about *the aura* (oooh) and *the dream* (ahhh). She was very excited that I would now have to admit that I had a connection. She wondered if the girl could be my "inner child" (the first time I had heard of the term), but I was really getting the name "Amy" in my head. Interestingly, Erin had pulled out a psychic workbook at 1 a.m. the same morning and, at the time, didn't know why. She now believed it was for me, so I agreed to drop by and pick it up later in the day.

On my way to Erin's, I stopped by a bookstore to check on the aura book the psychic had mentioned, as well as books on Disney World and potty training. I asked an employee for help in locating the spiritual books, and she directed me to the religion/inspirational section. It was immediately obvious that the book I was looking for would not be there. Luckily, the metaphysical/new age section was close by, preventing me from leaving under the assumption that the bookstore didn't carry "the weird stuff." I spent about forty-five minutes perusing this newly discovered category of material. Although I didn't find an aura book fitting the psychic's description, I spotted the words "How to Connect with Your Guide" in a book entitled *Opening to Channel: How to Connect with Your Guide* by Sanaya Roman and Duane Packer. Connecting with my guide seemed to be the message of the psychic and my dream, so I bought it. I also purchased three other books that I hoped would give the check-out clerk the perception that I was just a normal person and not some loony with this channeling stuff. My attempt at camouflaging the channeling book by purchasing other items was the same routine that many of us do when buying tampons or condoms. If you just buy tampons, they know you're having your period, and if you just buy condoms, they know you're about to have sex. Even if I wasn't successful in my disguise, at least I diffused my discomfort.

That evening I read the first quarter of the book, which was an introduction to channeling. The gist of this section was to confirm whether you were being led to, and were ready for, channeling. Everything I read called out to me. I couldn't put the book down. It was as if the authors knew my life and were affirming different stages and events that had transpired. I was sure that channeling was where I was supposed to be going—until I read the next section on opening to channel, which described what channeling actually was.

WHOA! Wait a minute. This definitely wasn't what I had in mind. I had not envisioned freeing up my body so that a spirit could enter me and use my body to communicate with others! What I had envisioned was that I would meditate and, in the process, allow my thoughts to be guided by spirits or angels. I would then listen to *my* inner voices and thoughts as guided. Actually, meditation was even a stretch for me, as I had never tried it, although I had a sense that it was generally commonplace and socially acceptable. Thoughts of being possessed and out of control pervaded my mind. I went to sleep that night uneasy with what I had learned.

THREE

The Path to Channeling

day three

Tuesday, May 7, 1996

When I spoke with Erin on Tuesday morning, I shared with her my sense that I was being led to channeling. Her reaction was not confidence building, but it was honest. Basically, she said that channeling was heavy-duty stuff and that she's heard of some weird things happening with it. But I couldn't keep from mulling over in my mind all the affirmations from the book, the psychic's messages, and my dream. I felt that these were signs or connections, all within a forty-eight-hour period, which I shouldn't ignore. Later in the day, I was overcome by a powerful revelation: *Channeling was the decision that would open doors for me and require courage*, not some movie idea that wasn't mainstream. I just knew it in my core. I was beginning to see the psychic's messages less like a Ouija board game and more as information that was applicable and real.

I called Trey at work, uncertain how he would react to my new insight. His initial response was of concern about my objectivity, as all of this was progressing so rapidly and unexpectedly. He suggested that I not rush into channeling and that I give myself more time to think about it. I shared with him that I was apprehensive as well, but not unsure, as I felt in my heart that this was where I was being led. Trey told me that he was comfortable with my following my intuition, which had led me down the right paths in the past, and that I should go for it. We both acknowledged that this was a huge step.

I should explain that Trey did not have a personal relationship with God, although he did believe in a higher power or creator that had no active role in our lives. I had always hoped that my faith would serve as a catalyst to a more personal faith for him. So far, it had not. Despite Trey's distance from religion, he always possessed total confidence and belief in me and respect for my beliefs, religious and otherwise, even when I doubted myself. The strength and stability of my relationship with my husband carried over into strength and stability in every other facet of my life. It further gave me the freedom and the courage to explore life, and grow, in ways that I might not have attempted without his support. I find it amazing what you can do with the security of knowing that even if you fail, your spouse, or loved ones, will support you. So although our only previous knowledge of channeling was that it was one of those outlandish "Shirley MacLaine things," Trey trusted my instinct and encouraged me to go forward with it.

I did not decide to pursue channeling on a whim, despite the lack of any concrete signs from God that He wanted me to evolve into some form of psychic. I was just an average, "earthly" mom who shopped at Target and got through each day like most other people, using my mind and my feelings as my guides. What I did possess, which may vary from many, was an openness to accept that the signs I received were real, as well as a willingness to follow those signs. I suspect most people would not have gone forward here as I did, but all I can say is that I was trusting my heart and intuition. I could have easily rationalized why I shouldn't proceed, but I released that comfort, the security blanket called my mind. Something beyond me was at work, and I sensed it and trusted it. There was also an element of fun and adventure, like putting puzzle pieces together without having a clue as to what the final picture would reveal.

Through the course of this day, my comfort with channeling grew directly with the heightened certainty I was feeling that this was my path. I committed myself to at least try channeling, but I had one huge reservation: Did this fit in with God, and if so, how? So I prayed about it.

That night I read on in the book *Opening to Channel* and learned that there were four preliminary exercises to do before attempting to connect with your guide. These prologue exercises basically progress from relaxation to meditation to trance. I proceeded with the first two exercises. I was thrilled with the ease with which I was able to "achieve a relaxed state" and "hold a focus and concentration," despite having no experience in such exercises. Upon reading the final two exercises before "connection," I learned that I would need two crystals, preferably a real quartz and an amethyst, to continue.

FOUR

The Hands

day four

Wednesday, May 8, 1996

WHILE RUNNING ERRANDS, I stopped by an educational store that sold rocks and fossils for our little rock collectors, and I purchased the two crystals recommended by the channeling book. That night I gathered the two stones and two plants, a potted, indoor plant and a gerber daisy from the backyard, all required for the third exercise, "attuning with life-force energy." This was an exercise in sensing the subtle vibrations or energies of other life forms, which would help open an awareness of the presence of a guide at a feeling, intuitive level.

Let me share something with you to put this exercise into my context. When my brother died, a secretary at my law firm gave me a small, purple stone. She told me that the stone might help me by giving me some positive energy. I thanked her for it, knowing she was genuinely concerned for my well-being; it was a kind gesture. But I couldn't help thinking, "How in the world could some rock make me feel better?

Very strange." In other words, except for visits to the ocean, where I feel open, creative, and peaceful and sense the magnitude of God's greatness, I had never felt particularly connected to nature, other than appreciating its beauty.

At the end of each exercise in the book, the authors include an "evaluation" paragraph that provides a sense of whether you've mastered the exercise and can move on. Here it is for "attuning with life-force energy":

> Evaluation: If you are able to sense these subtle vibrations, even slightly, even if it feels like you are just making it up, that is good. Proceed to the next exercise, Trance Posture and Position. If you can't sense anything, repeat this exercise at other times until you can.

So I proceeded with this exercise, very aware of my block to its success, but determined to sense something so I wouldn't have to repeat it. Here is what I made up, I mean, felt:

- quartz—smooth and soft, yet it vibrated
- amethyst—message "for the heart"
- gerber daisy—warm like the sun; my hand felt cold and tingly when I pulled it away
- potted indoor plant—not much; a little cold

Time to move on!

Now I was confronting the exercise "trance posture and position," the final exercise in preparing to connect with a guide. I found the word "trance" intimidating, as it brought forth images of the revival, charismatic churches where the parishioners scream out and talk in tongues.

The trance exercise was fairly detailed, so I read it several times to get a sense of the progression of steps; it's hard to relax totally when you're trying to remember what's next on the list. On the first attempt, I felt that I succeeded in getting to a relaxed state that I had not reached the day before. I was at a very comfortable and peaceful place that took a conscious effort to leave. I knew I was getting it, so I reread the exercise and tried again. This second time I focused on a particular image that I hadn't before, specifically from the book:

> Imagine all the cells in your right-brain, your receiving mind, reflecting perfectly the higher planes of reality, much like mirrors. Imagine the higher energy flowing from your right-brain into your left-brain, your conscious mind, with perfect precision and clarity.

With this image in mind, I naturally leaned my head to the left so that my right brain was higher and completely exposed at the top of my body. I visualized an energy or light coming down from directly above me in a confined ray, much like a spotlight, into my right brain. I then naturally leaned my head to the right, allowing the energy to flow to my left brain and ending with my left brain totally exposed to the light/energy spotlight. (If you're doing this "Valley girl" head movement as you read, I hope you find it humorous that many of my friends confessed to doing it as well.) Something was happening! I felt energy, tingling, warmth, and light-headedness. Intrigued by these new sensations, I repeated the left-to-right head movement and again felt the sensations at an even stronger level. I remained there for a moment, taking in the energy, familiarizing myself with it, and acknowledging it.

Once comfortable with this, I started the process again, leaning my head to the left, but this time something wild and totally unexpected occurred. *I had help.* I felt pressure on the back of each side of my head, as if there were hands grasping my head from behind. These "hands" pulled my head back and moved it to the right, taking me to a higher energy level and remaining there while my head "rested" on my right shoulder. Oh my God! This was wild! This was unbelievable! I feared my adrenaline rush would pull me out of the state, but it didn't. The hands guided me completely through the process another time, as if to make clear to me the exact movement I needed. Again I felt the warmth and tingling of the energy, but my heart was racing fast and furiously, which frightened me a bit. Although I was unsure whether my heart was racing from the energy or from knowing that something or someone had moved my head, I felt an urgent need to slow my heartbeat down. So I said "bye" and that I would try again soon. I "worked" my way out of this altered, trance state. My head was guided! My head was guided! I shivered uncontrollably as I recorded this event in my journal.

Trey came into our bedroom shortly after this and witnessed the highly stimulated state I was in. When I told him about the hands, he wanted to help me go further. We decided to proceed with the next exercise "ceremony of welcome to the guide's realm and first meeting with your guide." The title of this exercise also intimidated me because now I was knocking at the door of a completely unknown place. In addition, I was apprehensive about my ability to completely relax with Trey present. Despite my self-consciousness, I sensed that Trey was a part of this journey, and I knew that he needed to see it in order to understand it. I also felt that I'd have to get comfortable with other people's presence eventually, so why not now with my husband?

Trey and I both read the exercise. Because it was extensive, we decided to let Trey talk me through it. Although I did not feel the hands or feel as if I connected with my guide this time, I felt incredible energy. This energy pulled me upward. I was dizzy, yet relaxed. I remained there, energized, for a long while, aware of Trey watching me and waiting to see if anything else would happen. It didn't, so I worked myself out of the trance. Trey sensed my struggle to come out, and I was glad he could at least witness that. I later would learn that Trey sensed other things that he was uncomfortable sharing with me at this time.

The exercises this night brought forth an exciting breakthrough, but they also brought to light two significant concerns. The first concern is where the embarrassing part begins for me, and yet I know that it is important to share it with you. While in meditative trance, I received intense "spiritual energy." It was like being electrified; my whole body was in a state of vibration. And immediately afterward, my body shook uncontrollably, much like coming off an epidural after childbirth. I sensed that my body was releasing or shedding the energy it received during trance. A consequence of this receipt and release of energy was heightened sensitivity in my clitoris (okay, I said it!). I was wet and sexually stimulated. Needless to say, I was very uncomfortable with that sensation arising from something other than my husband and even worse, from something spiritual.

My second concern, however, weighed even more heavily on my mind. Whose hands were these? How were they connected to God? Was I headed down a path that would distract from or diminish my relationship with God? Was this God sanctioned? I felt that I needed some guidance on these questions before I could fully and wholeheartedly proceed with this new journey. Although I had turned to God in prayer the day before, so far I had not felt the heightened love that one might expect and that the channeling book extolled. I did, however, feel comfort, security, and peace while working on my connection. And I was receiving confirmations and, accordingly, gaining confidence that this was indeed my path of spiritual growth. But my concern and uneasiness about how this all fit in with God remained.

Because of my growing concerns, I decided that I should talk with someone familiar with channeling before going forward. I knew of one person, but only indirectly. While on a cruise in 1994, Trey and I had met a guy, Dean, who performed as a comedian on board. We struck up a conversation and learned that he wrote screenplays. We quickly connected with him and he with us because of our similar interest in movie writing.

The Hands

We spent a large part of the last few days of the cruise with Dean and in the process learned about his girlfriend, Elaine. Elaine is a spiritual advisor who uses a multitude of approaches: channeling, laying on of hands, astrology . . . . Dean seemed like this normal and nice guy, but he was living with this psychic lady, whose lifestyle wasn't so normal or mainstream. The contrast was intriguing, and Dean's stories of Elaine's work were fascinating. Dean and I kept in contact after the cruise, exchanging screenplays and letters from time to time, so Elaine seemed like the natural person to contact about my concerns. Of course, I continued to pray about them. At 1 a.m., I cranked out a letter summarizing all that had transpired in the past four days. I asked Elaine for her insight on how channeling was connected to God and on how it would affect my relationship with God. I never expected that those questions would be answered long before I heard from her.

FIVE

Contact!

day five

Thursday, May 9, 1996

First Meeting

I mailed my letter to Elaine with the hope of talking to her within a week. I intended to refrain from the channeling exercises until we had spoken. But I found that I couldn't get this channeling stuff off my mind. So when a rare opportunity presented itself to relax and feel the energy during the day on Thursday, I used it. My son had fallen asleep, and I had thirty minutes of free time before picking up my daughter from preschool. I set my oven timer and sat on the floor of my den. Since I didn't have time to work with the channeling book, I decided to relax and replay the head movements that the hands had moved me through the night before. I closed my eyes, relaxed, and focused on my breathing. Quickly, I felt energy. Then, as I did my side-to-side head movements, new and unexpected things happened. Here are my journal notes from this session:

I let loose and let him (my guide/the energy) move my head for me. There was lots of fine tuning like an antenna. Never saw light, always dark but felt tingly and higher. I heard a deep male's voice resonate in my body that said, "Hi Jenice." As the energy got stronger, I felt very sexually excited and acknowledged that. He told me to keep focusing on my head, which took a little effort. He told me to focus on my head again as I laughed about getting wet. I asked for messages to learn how to verbally channel. Instead of messages he moved my mouth and said, "I am . . . I am . . . ," and I was searching for a name and then I let go of that expectation. Then, through my mouth, he said, "I am your guide. I will help you." He told me mentally that we had done enough for now, and I said I didn't want to go yet (this place was very warm and comfortable). He said enough. So I brought myself out. When he spoke verbally, my mouth moved like the tin man's in *The Wizard of Oz*—shaky and rusty with vibration. The faintest whisper came out. I was fully cognizant of what was occurring and focusing on relinquishing control of my mouth. It was easy and fun! Fifteen minutes in and out and my first connection.

Incredible! All I did was relax and this happened! Last Sunday, only four days ago, I had no clue as to what channeling was, and now some spirit had talked to me and through me. Although I wondered why I was being summoned and where in the world this was going to take me, I was caught up in the moment and celebrated. I immediately called Erin to let her know that I had connected! As she had been with each step I'd taken, she was amazed and thrilled. This was the last time I spoke with Erin until Friday.

I am struck by this last sentence coming out the way it did, given that it was only one day later that I spoke with Erin again, but it illustrates a point. During the first few weeks of grieving over Craig's death, I lost all sense of time. I recognize that others' experiences with grieving may be different, but I found myself thinking that much more time was passing than actually was. It is as though there is a basic standard of thought or mental process that occurs in any typical day. While grieving, my mind operated in such high gear that the standard tricked or misled me into thinking significant time had passed, when in fact it had not. The same phenomenon was occurring now.

I can't begin to explain the extreme level of mental activity that was taking place. Suffice it to say that my mind was constantly working on anything and everything remotely connected to what I was experiencing: the events in my life leading to this, the characteristics about myself that enabled me to open up to this connection, the effects of this connection already in my life, the extraordinary consequences that this connection would have in my future, understanding the last exercise I had done and using that understanding to go forward with the next exercise, what my purpose or role would be with this gift, how my family and friends would react and how I would tell them, and on and on. My mind was now in spiritual mode, either receiving or reflecting, and I couldn't stop it, nor did I want to. So only one day would pass before I spoke with Erin again, but it was as if significant time had passed in a spiritual growth sense. I was in the process of being awakened in every sense.

Here are a few reflections from this day:

- My life has been a process of getting rid of my "earthly baggage" or negatives/barriers, such as insecurities, and I am now able to open up to the spiritual world.
- As with the psychic and now with my guide, I should not try to interpret the messages. Keep the messages in mind and allow the meanings to come naturally, that is, don't limit the messages within a particular context or expectation.
- I should trust my initial instinct or impression and not allow the passage of time or my logic to cause me to doubt the

subtleties and not-so-subtleties of the spiritual world. For example, when the force moved my head, I knew it wasn't me, yet the next morning I began to doubt that something like that could really happen.

- The psychic's message to keep a sense of humor is helpful with the sexual excitement side effect of the spiritual energy.
- I'm feeling more relaxed with the kids and able to handle their conflicts with less emotion and more patience and understanding. I'm feeling such joy in the little things, like their smiles and cute thoughts. In the past, I've been a "high-powered" mom, putting pressure on myself to work with my kids in an academic sense. I'm realizing that my focus should be more on teaching them about God and our purpose in life and on helping them to realize their full potential with respect to God's purpose for them.
- I am in a constantly energized state from the spiritual energy, like being on a stimulant. As a consequence, my needs for food and sleep have decreased dramatically. (I had lost three or four pounds since Sunday, which I neither intended nor desired, as I was already thin.)
- I need to have the TV and the radio off so there is silence within which to think and to hear my thoughts and inner voices.
- Although I have hoped to see light and/or feel an overwhelming sense of love as more clear signs of God's intent and part in this experience, I am feeling very comfortable and secure that this experience is focused on goodness.

Second Meeting

My preoccupation with this spiritual journey had distracted me from preparing for my son's third birthday at our home—just two days away. I used the mild panic that was creeping in to focus during the evening hours on the birthday party.

The kids and I proceeded to transform our home into a dinosaur jungle for a dinosaur safari party. At the risk of sounding corny, we had a magical time together. Although energized, I was in a very peaceful and relaxed state, atypical of my usual "perfectionist" mentality. My peacefulness allowed me to allow my children full participation, and they were ecstatic to play a part in the transformation. Trey had immediately sensed the energy in our home when he came home from work, and he told me so. We were all surrounded by and exuding a uniquely positive energy. The beauty of this energy reinforced both my intuition and Trey's that what was happening to me was in fact good, in a good-versus-evil sense. Even so, my concerns about channeling remained, and I continued to pray for insight.

That night a very close friend of mine telephoned. Her mother had died several months earlier, and she had been having trouble grieving. She called to thank me for my efforts to talk with her about her mom and to apologize for her unresponsiveness to my efforts. Of course, I neither expected nor needed her thanks or apology, but I was glad to hear that she was confronting her problems with grieving. She had been seeing a counselor for a couple of months, and together they had determined that my friend did not allow herself to feel sad. Unable to recall a time in her life when she had been sad, she felt she was incapable of feeling sadness. That was inconceivable to me because I have always felt my own pain, as well as others', so deeply. Although I had once felt burdened by how intensely I felt the world's pain, Craig's death had enabled me to use those feelings in a positive way by showing compassion to others who are hurting.

We acknowledged my friend's fear of allowing herself to feel the pain of her mother's death, knowing that a lifetime's worth of sadness could surface. We took comfort in the fact that she was aware of and addressing her issues with grieving, but we also knew that she had a long and painful road ahead of her. During this time, she was frequently in my prayers. After hanging up, I couldn't get it out of my mind that my friend did not allow herself to feel the emotion of sadness.

When the kids were in bed, I purposely turned *on* the TV to distract my mind so that I could address additional birthday matters. I was able to get much done. I finished up about 1 a.m. and then sat on our couch to pray before going to bed. I prayed to God to help my friend, to help me focus on Trey and his spiritual growth, as I was feeling selfish this week for being so self-focused, to help my connection with our kids deepen and grow, to help me get rid of my jealousies and envy, which I felt were my biggest negatives left to overcome, to know how channeling was connected to God, and so on.

I was praying from the heart, not merely reciting my prayers, as we all do at times. While praying so intently, I was pulled into channeling by my guide. I hadn't called my guide, but I was just there with him. I also felt the presence of two others: my friend's mother and my brother Craig. I cannot explain how I knew they were there, but I just knew. I wasn't thinking about what was happening, instead I was just in it, if that makes sense. I said hi to Craig and then asked my friend's mother what I could do to help her daughter. No verbal message was given, only a sense to trust my instinct in my help to her.

I allowed the energy I was receiving to direct and lead me. It pulled my head all the way back so that it rested on the back of the couch. For several seconds, the energy was tremendous, as if I were plugged into an electrical outlet and being charged. Although my whole body shook and vibrated aggressively, it was not painful or unpleasant. My head was then pulled back up straight, yet at the same time it felt heavy and slightly resistant to being lifted. With my eyes still shut, I saw light peripherally on my left and on my right. This was the first time I saw anything other than darkness, and even now most of the space was still dark, except for the light, or really more of a glow, on the outside of each eye. I noted that the light on my right was brighter. The only question I asked was whether this connection with the spiritual realm would hurt my relationship with God and Jesus.

Then, in the distance, I felt the presence of both God and Jesus. I didn't see Them, but I had the knowledge or awareness that They were with us, and I could also feel Their energy and essence. Then I sensed God leaving and my guide bringing Jesus closer to me. Jesus told me that I had prayed to help others and that I had a great purpose that would now evolve. I asked about not feeling the love, and He didn't answer or explain other than to say, "I love you." I took comfort in His words, as intellectually I knew that He did love me, but I still didn't *feel* the emotion of love, despite desperately wanting and needing to feel it. Then I sensed His wings coming from behind me and crossing at the tips in front of me. For a brief yet wondrous moment, I was wrapped in Jesus' wings. And then He was gone.

Energy maneuvered my head, pulling my left ear to my shoulder and then my right ear to my shoulder, repeatedly and quickly. I was given the awareness that I had two guides, one on each shoulder, in effect. The maneuvering continued for a significant period of time as if to allow me to compare their energies and know their differences. We didn't converse, but instead I simply was given general knowledge of who they are and what their purposes would be in working with me. Amy was on my left. She is the child that I met in my dream, and she is my creative guide. Her main purpose is to help me with my writing, although she is available for all my spiritual needs. And then there is my "high guide," who was on my right. He is highly evolved and wise. High Guide's energy is much stronger than Amy's. He is here to help me in my spiritual awakening and growth. He is my teacher and will help me in the discovery of spiritual truths, which I can then pass on to others.

After receiving the awareness of my guides and their roles, I was able to converse with them in my head. The fact that Amy was a child intrigued me. I told her that I've always had a strong connection to children, but that it felt odd, as a parent responsible for children, to have a child as a guide. Although I acknowledged that she possessed much greater knowledge than I, I still sensed that I had something to teach her. She answered that she would learn from me too. I asked if she would verbally channel through me, and she answered that we would do it all, which meant that we would not be limited to any particular method of communication. I then felt concentrated energy in my arms and hands as she fine-tuned that energy. She had me move each finger individually on both hands, and the energy soared within the particular finger that I moved. High Guide then dismissed me, and as I left them, I asked what to do with their energy, that is, whether to give it back or take it in. They said to take it in so that I could exist at, or be of, a state of greater light.

So I took in their energy, not that I needed it to be in the clouds! I had not only just met my two guides, but in response to my concern about channeling, I was brought within the presence of God and Jesus! And Jesus came to me and shared such beauty. He told me that God's purpose for me would be forthcoming. He told me that He loves me. And He hugged me. Dear God, how did I get here? Dear God, why me? Dear God, thank you!

I desperately wanted to share this incredible meeting with Trey, but it was after 2 a.m. and he was in a deep sleep. So I recorded this amazing encounter in the journal I had been using throughout this week: the *Plain and Simple Journal* created by Sue Bender. The last five days had been like being caught up in a whirlwind, especially the last twenty-four hours. As you can imagine, I was not able to fully absorb and assimilate what was happening, although having been in the presence of God and Jesus, I knew that this was truly a GREAT experience. Recording on paper what was happening enabled me to relax, knowing it was available for future reference, and to continue as a passenger on this journey.

I'm including the final two pages of journal notes on this evening's encounter so that you can see what I consider a *"Celestine Prophecy*

For a few moments I was back & forth to compare the energies. High guide definitely talked/answered my questions and verbally w/o me focusing on it - & can very fast - like I was distracted so easier to come. (Distracted b/c back & forth).

I told Amy how I thought odd she's a child b/c I've always felt connected to kids but more b/c although she was spirit & knew it all, I felt like a teacher to kids & to her. I asked if I was to help her too & she said she'd learn from me too. I asked if she would verbally channel & she said we'd do it all. I then felt energy in my arms & hands as she finetuned that energy. She had me move each finger too.

✻ I've been concerned & confused about not feeling the love & compassion I expected. I'm now sensing that although secure, I don't open to love from others & that is a big step/goal for me to accomplish - I must open myself to feel the love. (My love for myself is on a mental basis not emotional) Wow!

Also as coming out, I asked what to do with ~~my~~ their energy — throw it back or take it in. They said take it in — that is why I will exist or be of a greater light state.

> If we can listen and hear what is being offered, then anything in life can be our guide.

Wow!

Focus on my love of my kids when really feeling it & realize & acknowledge that's how God & guides feel about me coincidence." The picture and inspirational message depicted on these two pages are eerily on point, which I noticed immediately after making my entry. On the first page, two faceless people sit side by side, and on the adjacent page the message reads: "If we can listen and hear what is being offered, then anything in life can be our guide." WOW!

On these journal pages, you can also read about my concern and confusion over not feeling the love and compassion that I expected. For the first time, I was beginning to realize that there was something in me, or about me, that prevented me from accepting and feeling love. Although I did not have a clear sense yet of how or from where this barrier originated, I knew that overcoming it would require some hard work on my part. I wrote, "I Must Open Myself to Feel the Love." I decided to extrapolate from the strong emotional, unconditional love I felt for my kids to the awareness that God and Jesus and my guides loved me at least to the same degree.

SIX

Birth and Blossoming

day six

Friday, May 10, 1996

Soulmates

Although I typically require a lot of sleep, I awoke at 5:30 a.m., after sleeping just three hours. My body and mind were brimming with spiritual energy, but who's complaining! Trey stirred, and I couldn't help but engage him, as my mind was full of glorious news to share. In Trey's arms, I told him about the two guides who contacted me, introduced themselves, and delineated what their purpose and roles would be with me. I shared that my guides had brought God and Jesus to me and that I had been given an incredible interaction with Jesus, that Jesus had told me that my purpose would evolve, and that He loves me, and that before He left, He wrapped His wings around me.

I confessed that despite this incredible gift, I still did not feel the intensity of Jesus' love. At that moment, I realized that just as my friend could not feel sadness, I did not feel love wholly. A moment before, I had seen our conversation from the previous day as an opportunity to support her—now I realized that it was a gift to me.

As I spoke to Trey in those early morning hours, a window to my true self and my life began to open. It was clear that at some point during my childhood, I had started building a wall so that I wouldn't feel love. If I didn't feel love, I would have a defense protecting me from the pain of love lost or rejected or unreciprocated. John and Trey had chipped away at that wall. But instead of allowing myself to feel love on an emotional level, I relegated it to an intellectual level, so that I still had some protection. Naturally, this held true in how I felt about myself. Over my life I had built up a resumé of who Jenice was. I liked and respected her and thought that she was a pretty neat person, but I did not love her.

While conveying this, the floodgates opened, filling me with insights about myself, about Trey, and about our relationship. I was able to see so clearly and without conscious effort: I just understood. I was on automatic pilot, expounding the truth and essence of "us." Trey lay there in silence, taking it all in.

From early in our relationship, I had known somehow that Trey and I were meant to be. Two and a half years into our four-year courtship, I had acknowledged to God that I was committed to Trey for life, as if we were already married in God's eyes. I did this knowing that Trey was nowhere close to that awareness or commitment.

I also recognized that Trey's personality traits affected me in both positive and negative ways. Trey is a very strong and independent person. On the positive side, his strength gave me strength and his independence forced me to be independent. I grew from Trey's traits because of their paradoxical effect of encouraging me to be self-reliant, on the one hand, yet providing a crutch when I needed support, on the other. On the negative side, I sensed a withholding by him that was founded in his solid, self-reliant nature. His withholding felt like a lack of need for me or a failure to commit wholly at the soul level.

Although I knew in my heart that Trey loved me and would always be with me, I had allowed his withholding to tap into my fears, which I now saw for the very first time. I feared rejection and abandonment by the ones I love. When I added to those fears the insecurity that stemmed from my fear of being unworthy, I understood the root of my inability to accept and feel emotional love.

In seeing the reality of my fears, I was able to see the consequence of those fears in my relationship with Trey. I had closed off a part of my heart to him, not allowing myself to love him wholly, or to feel his love for me wholly, because I was too afraid of the possibility of being left behind and hurt. I had effectively created or perpetuated a small but real wall in my heart between me and my husband. Before the insight given to me on this morning, I had a nebulous, almost subconscious, awareness of that wall, which I couched in terms of "since Trey won't let me in all the way, I'm not letting him in all the way." I have since been given the knowledge that I created that wall through "assumption." Had I been secure and healthy with love, or aware of my own negatives and fears, I could have helped Trey long ago to see that we were soulmates and that God intended for us to be one with each other and with Him. Instead, I had fallen away from my own knowledge.

Now I saw our final barrier for what it was, without blame or fault, just limitations within each of us. For me, it was the fear of trusting Trey with my whole heart; I felt that I had to keep a piece of my heart for me to retreat to, a safe haven in effect, just in case he ever rejected me in the future. For Trey, it was his sense of self-sufficiency: He had never depended upon or needed anyone in his life, other than his mother, and he had created healthy, fulfilling, and successful personal and professional paths for himself basically on his own. Moreover, throughout Trey's life, people had depended upon and needed him, and he was very comfortable in that role.

I was not placing blame but merely sharing my feelings with love and honesty. With tears in his eyes, Trey acknowledged that I had pinpointed the barriers within each of us. He not only saw the truth in my words, but he felt that that truth elucidated the essence of our relationship. He confessed that he too had been vaguely aware of some of these things but had never dared to speak about them. He had assumed that because they touched the core of our relationship and of each of us as individuals, they were ingrained and thus unchangeable or untouchable. He was amazed that I was rattling off one truth after another with ease and honesty, especially upon waking at 5:30 in the morning!

We were both embraced in the beauty and clarity of the spiritual energy around us. Trey now recognized that this spiritual journey of awakening was not just mine, but ours. He knew that we were soulmates, as did I, in our new understanding of the term. We both recognized that God had brought us together for His purpose and that our souls were intertwined. Our personal and spiritual growth was a joint venture, and wherever we were going, we needed to go together. We both were ready for growth. We knew that to be wholly one with each other and with God, we needed to remove our remaining deeply embedded walls. By honestly acknowledging and confronting our own barriers, we had already begun the process of eliminating them and opening the door to the evolution of "us."

Our conversation continued with many other reflections about ourselves and the events of the week. One interesting thought Trey shared was his feeling that if I allowed myself to feel his and others' love, then I would see the light, God's light, that I had been waiting and wanting to see. When he stated this, I was overcome with a wave of comfort that he was right.

This morning had been such a glorious gift from God because for the first time in our relationship together, Trey and I had "spiritually connected." You might think that it would have felt vulnerable or threatening to be so completely open and honest, but instead it felt incredibly freeing. Although we walked through potentially painful grounds, we emerged on the other side having shed the pain and able to see more clearly the full beauty and unlimited spiritual potential of our relationship. We felt God with us, and we saw His hand in guiding us to realize the beauty and potential that He had designed for us. We were personally experiencing God's loving care for us . . . for Jenice and Trey! The beauty of this experience was so intense that it almost hurt. It is incredible to think that just a few days earlier, Trey did not believe that God was active in his life. And now he was seeing and feeling the awesome power of God.

Rebirth

Trey showered, and then as I showered, he left for work. I was struck by the irony of how we proceeded with our normal daily routines when we didn't feel "normal" anymore. Although externally nothing appeared different, I knew that both Trey and I were transformed internally, forever. I had been given an unsolicited gift of being with Jesus and God. I had met my two guides and learned of their purpose with me. I was awakening to the fact that receiving the love in my life was the journey of my life. And Trey and I had just reached a level in our relationship that neither of us had ever imagined reaching.

When I got out of the shower, I noticed that my face looked sunburned. This was very strange because I hadn't been out in the sun recently. Searching for an explanation, I wondered if it was possible that my face had turned red when I was with my guides and Jesus the night before. Although I hadn't seen any light, I had sensed that they were in a realm of intense light. As I studied my face in the mirror, a circular red splotch or rash about the size of a nickel appeared above each of my eyes, directly above my eyebrows, close to my nose. I know this is odd, but I instinctively knew that those two splotches represented my two guides. And it gets wilder. A small and very deep red circle, a little larger than a pencil mark, appeared in the center of my forehead. I immediately knew that this dot symbolized Jesus. Again, I can't explain *how* I knew any of this, yet I knew more surely the truth of these matters than I knew everyday matters that are readily verifiable.

I had been praying to know how my spiritual experiences from this week fit in with God, and that prayer was being answered. GOD (JESUS) WAS THE *CENTER*. God was also at the top of this pyramid or triangle and my guides were lower in the hierarchy, but I now knew for certain that they were within God's hierarchy. I had no doubt that my guides were given to me by God (Jesus). Needless to say, I freaked out a little seeing God address my concerns with channeling through physical evidence on my forehead. I kept staring in the mirror to make sure I really was seeing what I thought I was seeing. I desperately wanted to share this with Trey, but I knew he wasn't at work yet, so I decided to take a picture. I hesitated on my way out of the bathroom.

Standing naked in my bathroom, halfway between a white door behind me and a mirror in front of me, I wondered if I could see my own aura. I tried, focusing on my eyes and forehead. But instead of my aura, I saw, with my eyes open, a white glow around the crown of my head that grew in intensity to look like a halo. Trey was right! I was newly aware of my barrier to feeling love, and accordingly to seeing the light, and now I was literally seeing the light. I was exuberant.

God was not done with me yet. A bright white light appeared on the outskirts of my face. This light slowly bathed my whole face, coming over from the sides and down from my forehead, filling every indentation and curvature of my face like a fitted glove. This light was different from any light I had ever seen. It had a deep, intense brightness, yet I did not need to shield my eyes or squint to look at it. It had depth and density, yet it was transparent. It possessed the characteristics of cleansing and holiness, if you can imagine light possessing such traits. The light seemed to be a part of me. I don't know if I was exuding the light from within or if it was penetrating me from without, but it was another layer of my face. This great light moved down my face and neck to my shoulders, and then . . . I was with Jesus. I honestly don't know if I had shut my eyes or not. But I was standing before Jesus and seeing Him in all His glory with my own eyes, not through an image or impression in my mind. He was suspended high and tall and large, above and in front of me. He was showing me His brilliant light, and I thanked Him wholeheartedly for allowing me to see it. My heart exalted in witnessing the magnificent beauty of Jesus and His light.

I have to admit that, even now, my encounter with Jesus remains somewhat ineffable. While with Jesus in His spiritual realm, I encountered experiences that do not normally occur in our earthly realm. Consequently, I find myself challenged to pull out the precise word or exact analogy that conveniently describes these encounters. One example of this challenge is in describing certain experiences of all those I had with Jesus, which I categorize as "pure" experiences.

Although our usual understanding of "pure" as utter or absolute is helpful, I feel our earthly experience of pure cannot sufficiently describe my spiritual experience of pure. Here is my attempt at describing my pure experiences with Jesus:

If we isolate any moment in our lives, we see that during that moment we were conscious of some combination of the elements of emotion, belief, awareness, experience, and so forth. For example, when I am sad, I am conscious not only of my sadness, but also of other feelings or experiences, some of which relate to my sadness and some of which do not. Despite my prevailing sadness, I can still laugh at a joke or carry on a conversation on other topics. However, during my pure experiences with Jesus, I did not have access to other feelings and experiences.

Normally, we could view the soul as a rainbow of innumerable colors of light, each color representing a different emotion, belief, awareness, or experience. "Pure" in the spiritual sense means that the soul is all one color of light, one experience, one consciousness: all, complete, whole. During my pure experiences, only Jesus could move me to another state because there was nothing else in me; all I knew was the experience of the moment, and it was all consuming. I had no ability to leave my pure experience and move on, no other paths to take, no conscious thought other than the one thought Jesus placed in me. It was all my soul was at that moment, and my soul was experiencing the consciousness of that pure state completely. *I experienced wholeness in each experience of oneness.*

The spiritual experience of pure is captured by this "wholeness in oneness." Each of my pure experiences was whole in that I experienced only a single consciousness and I experienced all facets of that single consciousness. In other words, a pure experience is whole in that it *excludes* everything but that one experience and *includes* everything about that one experience.

From this magnificent encounter of seeing Jesus and His brilliant light, I was placed in my first pure state: the experience of my nakedness. All I saw was my naked body standing in pure light. All I felt was the shame of my nakedness. I desperately wanted to cover myself. I even tried, but Jesus did not let me. He comforted me by letting me know that the shame I felt was not through my own fault but was derived from Adam and Eve's "original sin."

In the moment after Jesus explained my shame, I was pure confession. I confessed my sins without mental thought; I just confessed as if Jesus had provided the list for me. I have elected to keep my confessions private, except for my first one, which upon later reflection surprised me because, although true, I was not aware that it was a sin. I confessed to disliking my body. Only through Jesus' giving me pure knowledge of my sins could I confess to Him the sin of disliking my body. I feel it is significant that this was the first of my confessions, as I explore further in Part II of this book.

Jesus then removed me from confession and placed me in pure "I'm sorry," pure remorse. I was sorry through every cell of my being. The pain of my sorrow consumed me with a brutal intensity that was unrelenting. I wept hysterically in my suffering and cried out "I'm sorry" over and over and over . . . . I longed to be perfect like Jesus, *for Jesus*, in both body and soul, and the pain of not being perfect was almost unbearable. I feel that I was in this pure state the longest, probably because of the depth of my anguish. I cannot fathom remaining there for eternity, although I know I could not have left remorse without Jesus giving me my next pure state. Afterward, I wondered if hell is being in a pure state of remorse.

I was then given the pure experience of purity. Jesus revealed to me His mercy and grace by removing my sins. He forgave me for my wrongdoings. He told me that I was good and pure. He again comforted me, this time with the knowledge that I could not be perfect. He said that I should be aware of my imperfections but not feel guilt about them. Specifically, Jesus told me, "Guilt is a barrier to growth, but awareness is an impetus for growth. You must strive for perfection yet be accepting of your faults."

And then I gave my will to Jesus. I just gave my life to Him without contemplating what I should do next or even considering whether I was ready to give my will to Him. I understood that my soul was aligned with Him, that He was truth and love, that He was my source and creator, and that I wanted and needed Him to direct and guide my life. With this, my pure experiences ended, although I remained with Jesus longer.

Jesus unfolded my purpose. Simply, I am to help others in their spiritual journeys by helping them to understand what our purpose is in life. Jesus did not give me the answer to life's purpose, merely the tools to discover the answer so that I could pass on what I learn.

Now that I had my conscious thought again, I was aware that my bodily fluid was dripping from me into a puddle below me. I asked Jesus about sex because I felt that sex had a negative connotation on earth. Although He said nothing more than "Enjoy, enjoy," I received greater understanding from His response that I will share later.

I acknowledged to Jesus that I had not consciously *decided* to give Him my will, but that was what I had done and it felt very different than I had expected. I had always assumed that when you gave your will to God, you would relinquish control of your life. But in fact I felt the opposite; I felt empowered knowing with certainty the path I was to take now. I was still the same person with the same life, but Jesus had given me *direction* and *purpose*. I knew that I would exercise *my* mind and God-given gifts to do His will.

That's all that giving our will is: accepting what God's great purpose is for us, not necessarily lifestyle changes, just direction. We couch this transition in our lives in terms of "giving up" or "relinquishing" our will to God, when it might be more accurately described as "exercising our own free will" in choosing to fulfill God's higher purpose for us. Although this may seem like a mere semantic distinction, I was struck by the tremendous sense of empowerment, freedom, and fulfillment that I immediately felt. My soul was ready to do God's work, and He knew it.

Jesus hugged me with His wings for the second time. I allowed myself to feel His love more strongly this time, but I was aware that I was still denying myself the full beauty and power of His love. How I longed for Jesus to remove my barrier from me! He could have, but He didn't, because He was allowing me to clearly see the scope of my own limitation. In that moment of self-awareness, I understood the magnitude of my self-denial and barrier, and I knew that I had so much to gain from removing it myself. I laid my head on Jesus' wing and cherished the moment.

Jesus then asked me if I wanted to fly, and I was thrilled, "Yes!" Although I could not see our flight, I felt my body dangle below Jesus as He swiftly flew me higher and higher. When we stopped, I felt the presence of many spirits: High Guide, Amy, Craig, whom I thanked, my friend's mother, and many more unknown but joyous spirits. I was unable to see them, yet I was aware that they were all gathered closely in a crescent shape with me at the focal point. There were so many spirits that I couldn't begin to estimate the number. I confirmed with High Guide that he was present, and he verbally (through my mouth) responded, "Yes." And then I asked Amy the same question, and she answered mentally (through my mind) that she was.

I was aware that this gathering was for me. This was my welcoming committee to the spiritual world. It was analogous to a celebration of a birthday in that it was a celebration of my birth into the spiritual world, while on earth. Their joy consumed me. And as I stood before them filled with their joy, I knew that they were celebrating their accomplishment too. Together we had succeeded in establishing a direct and invaluable bridge between the spiritual and physical worlds. High Guide told me that I had come a long way very quickly and that they were all proud of me. He verbally channeled "Good, quick pace." I asked if I would still be able to write movies, and he answered that I would write great things. And then I was back on earth.

Back On Earth

I had just experienced in life what seemed impossible to experience until death. I stood naked before Jesus (God) and bared all, my entire being, body and soul. I was given the greatest gifts imaginable: utter knowledge that God exists, that Jesus is God, and that our souls live on after death. How can I fully convey the impact of this experience? From that moment on, I had absolute knowledge of God's existence, 100 percent knowledge and 0 percent doubt. My faith was transformed into knowledge! The strength inherent in this knowledge is what gives me the courage to "tell the world."

And as if that were not enough, I was given other gifts: forgiveness, knowledge of my purpose, and my awakening to discover the purpose of life. I would soon learn that I also had been given the gift of "spiritual eyes," or insight, for a brief time after this. In some ways, this was truly overwhelming. All of this was given to me—just an everyday person living life like many others—without any apparent explanation for why I was chosen.

Two intriguing impressions from this experience remain with me. First is the feeling that I was tricked or manipulated, in a positive way, into my meeting with Jesus. In my wildest dreams, I never would have imagined it possible to have an experience of baring all to Jesus, so, understandably, I would not have set up the circumstances needed. I was naked, having just showered, Trey was gone, and the kids were asleep. Jesus placed physical evidence on my forehead, which definitely caught my attention, and I was wanting to see light, so He gave me light, with my eyes open. And then I was just there with Him and my pure experiences.

Second is the position of my body during the experience. I stood with my feet spread shoulder-width apart, my arms out from my sides at about five and seven o'clock, palms forward, and my head raised to see Jesus. This was not a natural position to stand in, but one that I was placed in. My body was as open to Jesus as it could be for baring all. I was not permitted the comfort or security of bringing my arms to my sides or wrapping them around myself to shield my nakedness. A baby newly out of the womb is comforted when coddled or wrapped in a blanket. A child often instinctively withdraws into a fetal position when extremely upset. I longed for these comforts as I stood before Jesus with the pure consciousness of my nakedness. But I was forced, or maybe it was necessary for me, to remain bare and open.

I understand the curiosity that my experience provokes in others and that some people will want to know the details of what Jesus looked like and what I actually saw of Him. Unfortunately, I have little to share. I think I have put an expectation on myself to recall the details and am frustrated with the lack of them, but I saw no more than what I was allowed to see. Although I will try to describe what I saw and sensed as well as I can, I do not feel that there is any great significance to these recollections. My interaction with Jesus was through my soul, not my limited earthly eyes and ears. In other words, I was given knowledge and awareness within my being, so that visual or physical confirmation was not necessary. My spirit had shed my body, allowing a richer, more encompassing experience than my bodily senses would have allowed. As a result, not only was I unable to focus on visual details, but they were also inconsequential.

After the glove of light covered my face, I was instantaneously standing before Jesus, looking up to His immense being, which was much larger than human form. I knew that He was Jesus not by looking at His face, but rather through the awareness given me. He did have a face, although it wasn't defined in my vision. His entire being shone with a brilliant white light, and He was surrounded by white light. He had wings that spread a great distance out to each side, and they seemed to be His arms rather than wings attached to His back as angels often are depicted. I sensed He was a merging of two forms, a great white dove and a human body, although I couldn't see His body, as He wore a full-length robe of white light.

In my pure states, I saw and sensed only the particular emotion. With pure nakedness, it was as if I were seeing myself from above, out of my body, with white light filling all space. The parts of my body that I dislike seemed exaggerated in their imperfection. Pure confession and pure remorse were inner focused, with nothing visual. I don't remember anything visual with forgiveness, either, so I guess I was still inner focused, although I remember feeling as if I were, or was seeing myself as, a clean slate.

Both when I gave Jesus my will and when He revealed my purpose, I saw the same vision of Him as before, suspended high and tall and large, above and in front of me. And then I saw only my naked dripping body among whiteness immediately before I inquired about sex. When Jesus hugged me, both the night before and on this day, I didn't see His wings with my eyes, but a visual image of wings appeared in my mind. Yet I physically felt the softness of His feathers around my arms as well as on my cheek when I laid my head on His wing.

My flight up to my welcoming committee was in darkness. Jesus grasped me on the top of my shoulders, yet I had no sense of what body or bird part lifted me. My arms and body literally dangled as we flew and, although my body was standing in my bathroom, I felt my legs dangle too. At my celebration, I remained in darkness, although I had a picture in my mind of the numerous spirits in a crescent configuration. I remember moving my head from one side to the other as if I was looking at and taking in all the spirits. I was able to recognize a few in the process.

"Spiritual Drug" Highs And Lows

The first thing I did after my meeting with Jesus was to write it down. I felt a sense of urgency to capture every feeling, thought, and experience that had occurred since I awoke that morning while it was fresh and I was still in it. I grabbed a robe and my journal from my bedroom, and then I sat on a chair in the bathroom and wrote. There was so much. I was emotionally drained and overwhelmed, and yet I was energized and high. During my journaling, my son ran into the bathroom with the most tremendous smile and excitement. Although I didn't tell him what had happened, he seemed to be sensing the magnificence of my Divine encounter. He sat in my lap while I hugged him, and we shared our mutual excitement. Surprisingly, I was able to get him back to sleep shortly afterward so that I could finish my notes. After getting the basic information down, I realized that the two splotches and the center dot were still on my forehead, though starting to fade. I rushed to take a picture. Regrettably, although not unexpectedly, as I could only hold the camera at arm's length away, the picture turned out blurry and overexposed.

I called Trey to share with him what had happened. Can you imagine calling your spouse at work to tell him or her that you just had a visit from Jesus in your bathroom?! And just as wild, your spouse actually believes you?! Needless to say, this conversation definitely was not a typical one. Yet, just a couple of hours earlier, Trey and I had spiritually connected and he had recognized the effect of God's direct involvement in his life, both for the first time. So with the benefit of these experiences, he openly accepted my encounter with Jesus. He was in awe and ecstatic. He was also relieved to know for certain that this journey was given to us by God. *Thy will be done.* We were both exultant.

Immediately after talking with Trey, I called Erin. I asked her to come over to my house, for I had news that I wanted to share in person. She said that she would be over in the early afternoon. The wait was torturous because I was overflowing with excitement and felt as if I might burst. I literally skipped and danced around my house, like a child on her birthday, unable to restrain my rejoicing and celebration. I felt like I was on a drug, a spiritual high, and my being exuded the sheer joy and excitement of my new life. I was high and flying.

And then I came face to face with my first downer, a simple chore: I had to go to Sam's Warehouse Club to get items for my son's birthday party. I was having an extremely difficult time focusing mentally, and the thought of having to run an errand burdened and drained me. This may sound like an exaggeration, but it's not.

I was in a "higher realm," and I felt lighter, freer, and unburdened by worries and demands. I think that I was experiencing a deeper connection to my spirit than to my mind and body. I had no appetite and was even unable to taste the food that I forced myself to eat. The honeydew melon that were so sweet the day before was now tasteless. I sensed that earthly matters would suck me back into the earthly realm, as they required focus and attention to be accomplished. It was as if my mind were being pulled back into play, and it felt like a cage or prison to my spirit. The thought of leaving this spiritual plane depressed and frustrated me, and yet, because the demands of daily life cannot be avoided, I knew that it would be necessary for me to experience the low of coming off this "spiritual drug." I sensed that I would experience spiritually induced highs and lows in the future and would have to acclimate myself to them. The retreat from my high would not feel good, though.

So at noon, I dropped my daughter at preschool and then headed for Sam's. There, I searched strangers' eyes for an acknowledgment of this new person that I was. Others *had* to be sensing something wonderfully spiritual in me. But as far as I could tell, they didn't. Unbelievable! Another downer. On my way home from Sam's, a title to a book, "My Spiritual Journey of a Lifetime in One Week," popped into my head. I then knew not only *that* I would share my experience with others, but also *how* I would share it.

Throughout this day, my mind constantly received information, as if I had tuned into a radio broadcast from the spiritual realm. I couldn't write it down fast enough, but I recorded what I could. I disliked ignoring the kids, although they enjoyed a day full of public TV and videos. At home, I carried a notepad around with me and wrote, wrote, wrote. In the car, I wrote on scrap paper and school art work from the floor of my car. I was in receiving mode, and I went with it.

I marveled at the distance traveled in a mere six days, from earthly plane to spiritual plane. I had no clue whether there was more to come or this was it. Nor did I know whether the physical and psychic stimuli I was experiencing were permanent or temporary, and if temporary, how long they'd last. Only time would tell.

Sharing With Erin

When Erin arrived, I immediately saw a unique light in her eyes, which I also saw in my own on this one glorious day. Typically, when I look into someone's eyes, I see the color or lightness or darkness of their eyes and nothing more. Today, what I saw foremost was the reflection of light: a sphere of light next to the pupil that shone like a ray as it reflected. The significance of seeing eyes differently eluded me, but it was captivating. Erin's light was brilliant.

Although I enjoyed sharing the experiences of this week with Trey, I greatly appreciated the opportunity to share them with Erin, as she brought a wisdom to them that Trey and I did not possess. Sharing with Erin was like consulting with a spiritual teacher or counselor. Unlike most of us, who "awaken" to our journeys later in life or never at all, Erin was aware throughout her life of the spiritual nature of her journey. She is so in tune, in fact, that her life has been sprinkled with direct encounters with God, Jesus, and angels, experiences most of us find difficult to grasp.

I was able to tell Erin about my meeting with Jesus with comfort, ease, completeness (except for the sexual part), and uninhibited emotion. How wonderful for me! I was uncomfortable with the prospect of telling my extended family and other friends, afraid that they would conclude that I had lost my sensibilities. The opportunity to tell all to Erin (and Trey) was a tremendous relief and release for me, as I think it would be almost maddening to experience an epiphany and not have someone with whom to share it.

As I was overwhelmed by my miraculous encounter, I was grateful for Erin's enlightened analysis. Here are some of the insights she shared with me:

- Jesus gave me a gift of love during life that had previously seemed possible only upon death: the opportunity to stand *face-to-face* with Him, bare my sins, and be forgiven by Him. This experience would allow me to rid myself of the negatives of guilt and unworthiness, so that I might now open up to God's love and others' love for me.
- She suggested that I think of Jesus as a parent who loves me so unconditionally that He would allow me, His child, to suffer through confession and remorse, so that I could be exalted to a place of peace and joy afterward.

- She said that the dot that appeared in the center of my forehead is known as a "third eye," which is the energy center of our spiritual sight. My priest also confirmed this.
- Just as I had received a title with awareness that I was to write a book about this week's journey, Erin, as a pre-teen, had received a title to a religious paper that she was to write for school. Interestingly, Erin felt she must have channeled her report, as she did not remember writing it, despite having a finished product in her own handwriting.
- Erin advised me that I needed to pay close attention to maintaining my health while at this higher spiritual plane because my guides either could not or would not help with that. She had recently come across an allegory that she shared to illustrate her point: Would you consider a woman who gave away all of her belongings in order to do God's work a short-sighted or far-sighted individual? My answer was a short-sighted individual, knowing that at some point she would be pulled away from her purpose in order to regain and maintain her own basic necessities. She would need some of her material possessions as a security net to fully and effectively fulfill her mission.

Erin's advice hit home, as I was feeling no hunger and I was getting little sleep. Although at the time I did not fully understand why those physical changes were occurring, or why my guides would not instruct me to take care of myself, I recognized that I needed to be mindful to nourish myself. Even so, following through with Erin's sound instruction was difficult. Eating was burdensome and unappealing since I felt highly fueled by the spiritual energy. I ended up losing ten pounds in a week and a half before I was able to eat again and stop the weight loss. What my extended family saw was this energized, shrinking person, and they genuinely worried that I was going to have a mental breakdown. Both Trey and I knew that I was fine, but we were unable to convince either of our mothers of that fact. I became pregnant three weeks after meeting with Jesus, which quickly resolved any concerns with insufficient sleeping and eating. I'm sure at some point in my life I'll be begging for this spiritual weight-loss program!

As my dear friend and I sat in my study, we shared our most personal and intimate feelings about God's purpose for each of us in this life. I thanked Erin for being a catalyst in my opening up to God. Together, we cried like babies. I wept from the intensely overwhelming emotion of being with Jesus. Erin cried from the profound beauty of it. We knew that my life's journey was to be one of love, peace, and joy. What a blessing!

Psychic Abilities

For several days after being with Jesus, I remained at a higher spiritual plane. As a consequence of this altered state, I experienced remarkable abilities and insights. As an example, I could easily communicate with my guides at all times and in all places. It was as if High Guide, Amy, and I were constantly on the phone together. They would even initiate topics of conversation to direct me down new and different paths of discovery. While our connection was so direct and strong, I received, or was guided to, several "revelations." These revelations addressed the essence of our spirits as well as the purpose of our existence and our journey on earth. Many of these truths were revealed when I was writing and Amy would step in to finish my thoughts. In Chapter Seven, I have included examples of my notes where Amy cowrote or coauthored revelations.

Amy used this day, the sixth day of my week-long journey, to coordinate our writing connection. When she wanted to practice, I would feel a surge of energy in my arm and hand. I worked on releasing my control as she worked on finding the control. She intervened several times during my note taking for her exercises. I've enclosed one example of our scribbling.

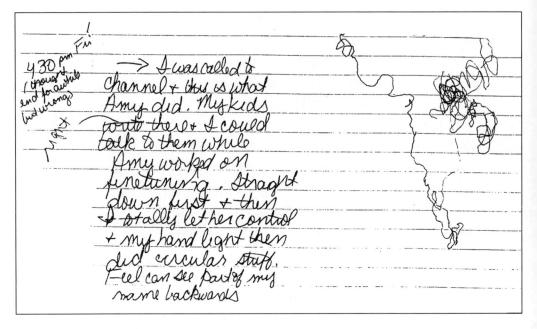

It appears to me that she wrote at least the beginning of my name, "Jen," in mirror image. The wildest part about this process was that when she summoned, I was able to give her my arm and she could do her thing without any mental participation on my part. In fact, as she practiced fine tuning the control of my hand, I was able to converse with my kids and even referee their arguments.

As awesome as our open line of communication was, I marveled even more over another gift that I attained. I referred to this gift earlier as "spiritual eyes." My spiritual eyes enabled me to see the truth, the core, the reality, of the world around me. I felt like I was removed from my limited earthly perspective and perched in a higher realm, allowing me to objectively watch the dramas on earth. I was able to see the underlying dynamic of relationships within my family and without. I was able to see personal issues of family and friends that were not clearly evident to them. The most dramatic ability arose in connection with our children. I was able to see the essence of each child, as if I had x-ray vision into their souls. Further, I could see their emotions and understand why they had them and from where they originated, and I knew the exact response needed from Trey and me to help them. This was not intuition but knowledge of my children and their feelings. As one welcome benefit of this gift, we solved our son's potty-training on this day.

Within a few weeks after my meeting with Jesus, I was back down to earth, altering the psychic abilities I had been experiencing. The method in which I channeled my guides changed significantly. I had also lost my spiritual eyes for the most part, although I continued to have moments of spiritual clarity. At the time, I did not know that that gift would be short-lived. I was hoping it was a permanent answer to my prayer "help me to be the best mom that I can be." And although I greatly lament its loss, I recognize how fortunate I am to have had that brief glimpse into my two older children. I have that gift forever. And it made a life-changing difference with respect to the relationship between our son and daughter.

My husband and I already had a good sense of our daughter's identity, and our intuition was confirmed on this day. She has a strong will and a commanding presence. She is highly motivated, very bright, and a sophisticated thinker. Her strength, confidence, and tenacity can be a pain in the behind at times, but those traits highlight her potential for making a positive difference in this world when it is her time and she is ready. The intriguing part is that she was prepackaged, as this description fit her on the day she was born, it fit her at four and a half years of age when this experience occurred, and it will remain true of her at seventy years old. Interestingly, my husband is also a prepackaged soul.

Our son, like most souls, was not prepackaged, just like his mother. We saw him like a piece of wet clay—soft and malleable. He is goodhearted, sweetly sensitive to both people and animals, inquisitive, and also very intelligent. Trey and I appreciated the beauty in both of our children. We also respected, and were comfortable with, their different personalities: our daughter's was more forceful and our son's was gentler. Although we were aware that our son was often overshadowed by the stronger presence of his older sister, we were not aware of the potential danger of that dynamic until this day. At one point, my son had a sock in his hand to put on before leaving for his playgroup. He wrapped the sock around his neck. In that instant, I received a horrifying vision. I saw my son, at three years old, with a rope around his neck, as he held the remainder of the rope above his head, strangling himself.

I can't begin to describe the terror I felt. I was petrified. I was shocked. I wanted to deny and suppress the image, as if I hadn't seen it. But I had. My fear then turned into rage; if all this spiritual stuff was leading me to foresee tragedy in the future, I wanted nothing to do with it! I had no concept of where I was being led spiritually, but how *dare* they show me my child committing suicide!

I know it seems improbable, but I was finally able to set this image aside for a while. I think that when we are confronted with the painful, we often seek to deny the pain by creating a different, false reality or by manipulating the pain into something less painful. I'm reminded of the drive to the hospital after the call that my brother Craig was there and that we needed to come immediately. I "knew" Craig must be dead, because we were never summoned after his other epileptic seizures, but I didn't want to accept that painful outcome. So during the drive, I desperately searched for another reason that we had to go to the hospital. Although I could not come up with any plausible reason, I accepted untenable ones. I was doing the same thing with the vision of my son, avoiding the reality in order to avoid the pain. I decided that I wouldn't tell Trey about this image.

At my son's playgroup, I felt more comfortable playing with the children than visiting with my "mom" friends on this day. I was exhausted and foggy, and talking with the kids took less energy and focus. Only one friend sensed something different about me, and she assumed something was wrong. Of course, I looked like hell and couldn't seem to speak coherently, so why wouldn't she?

Sharing With Trey

When Trey arrived home from work, we had so much to share with each other. Luckily, both the kids attended a "kids' night out" at our town's athletic club, so Trey and I could revisit our day with uninterrupted conversation. We were scheduled to attend a dinner at our church, but I knew I couldn't do it; I was mentally and physically spent. The only other time that I truly felt incapable of socializing was after Craig's death. Trey's excitement, however, rejuvenated me enough to celebrate and rejoice with my soulmate.

Trey revealed that he was profoundly changed by our conversation that morning and my encounter with Jesus and that on the drive home from work he had committed his life to serving God. This transformation in my husband was incredible to me. Over the course of this week, all of these remarkable events were happening to me, yet Trey was understanding them, accepting them, and feeling them. I was, and continue to be, immensely grateful to God for this. I have no concept of where our relationship would stand had God not pulled Trey into the experiences of this week, although I know it would be something far less than what it is now.

I am also grateful to Trey for his willingness to open his heart to God. From his lifelong perspective that God is not active in our lives, he easily could have denied what was happening. Instead, he was in it and experiencing God along with me. And now he had given his will to God and had asked God, our active source and creator, to direct and guide him according to His plan. Trey's transformation is a testament to the power and splendor of God's spirit when we open ourselves to receiving Him.

Trey and I both felt so open and alive. We were wholeheartedly willing to go down any and every path that Jesus directed us down, including channeling. Before my meeting with Jesus, I had had two concerns with channeling. We were so thankful that Jesus had answered both concerns.

My first concern dealt with whether channeling was "good" in a religious sense. I knew that channeling was not a practice recognized by Christianity, and I sensed that it would arouse concern, maybe even fear, in many Christians. I had been feeling the strain of going against religious, and societal, approval. So naturally, I had prayed for God to let us know whether He sanctioned channeling. We now were completely certain of the inherent goodness of our new path, for Jesus had personally and directly answered our prayers. Jesus allowed me to meet with Him in person, He disclosed His purpose for me, and He revealed that my guides were His spirits given by Him as conduits to fulfill my spiritual purpose. I cannot imagine a greater sign of the goodness of our journey.

Tonight I learned that my second concern was also shared by Trey. This concern dealt with the heightened sexual sensitivity. On Thursday, I had mentioned my sensitivity to Trey, but he had not shared his with me. He now told me that on Wednesday evening while helping me with the channeling exercise, he also felt energy in his groin. I assume it is understandable how our physical response would cause us to doubt a higher spiritual purpose in channeling. Rationally, it made sense that we would feel energy in our sexual organs, as they are the most sensitive parts of our body. Yet, before my encounter with Jesus, neither of us was comfortable relying on that logic to conclude that we were receiving a positive spiritual energy, rather than a possibly negative energy. Jesus had dismissed this concern with His response, "Enjoy, enjoy," to my question about sex, as well as with the awareness He gave me in that moment about human sexuality. In fact, as Trey and I talked of this former concern, High Guide suggested that we go make love—and we enjoyed!

Sex

Upon sharing a draft of this book with family and friends, I discovered that many were disturbed by the sexual aspect of my experience.

Several people have asked why I don't just delete it. This is a valid question deserving of an answer.

First, I think it would be beneficial to further explain the physical stimuli I received as I connected more directly to the spiritual energy. One friend described her experience with spiritual energy as similar to drinking a cup of coffee on an empty stomach. It also could be likened to being in a prolonged state of an adrenaline rush. These two descriptions accurately portray the energy I received through the normal course of the day during this week. But during my meditative states, the energy I received was significantly stronger. The best way I can describe this phenomenon is that it felt like I was plugged into an electrical outlet. My body literally vibrated and mildly convulsed, causing my sexual stimulation.

For a time after my channeling connection was established, I continued to receive greater and greater surges of energy. I sensed that my guides were taking me to higher and stronger planes of energy as if I were ascending stairs, allowing my body to become acclimated to the energy with each step. For whatever reason, I could not jump directly from the earthly plane to the spiritual plane that they desired me to reach.

This is how our channeling sessions progressed: Originally, I started at ground zero. To get to the first plane, I followed the exercises in the channeling book and received strong "electrical" energy. The next time I meditated, I began at that first plane without going through the exercises, or feeling the energy, previously required to get there. Instead, I was directed through different exercises and felt new energy in reaching the second plane. When I meditated again, I started at the second plane without the necessity of retracing my steps, and so on. Eventually, I was able to raise my energy directly to High Guide's and Amy's energy planes without experiencing the energy surges.

In effect, my body became accustomed to the energy through gradual steps of exposure. Now, for the most part, I do not experience energy surges and, accordingly, I rarely have the sexual stimulation.

When my body does respond to the energy, I am comfortable with it, as I know it is a natural physical response to the energy received. I also know that my sexual stimulation has no relevance to the message or essence of my spiritual experiences and that I am not receiving negative or evil energy.

Curiously, when I shared my experiences of this week with my priest a few months later, he was not concerned with this physical response, and he told me that it was both predictable and normal with meditation. He also believes that a sexual response may arise as an integral part of the "ecstasy" of an encounter with God, rather than merely as a by-product of the strong spiritual energy.

My reason for including this information is twofold. My hope is that after learning about my experiences, others will open up to their own spiritual connection. If the sexual stimulation happens to occur, they will at least be aware of this potential side effect, understand that it is normal for some, and not preclude themselves from further growth because of it. From a practical standpoint, it can also serve as an indicator that they are receiving energy.

More important, I feel the need to share every part of my experience, as every part has significance. This encounter was a gift to me from God, largely given for the purpose of sharing with others. I know that God will reach different people through different aspects of my experience. As I cannot deny the experience or question its purpose, I cannot choose to delete awkward or embarrassing aspects of it. And I cannot change the experience. It was what it was.

Finally, I was asked by a single woman why I asked Jesus about sex and its negative connotation when I professed to having a great marriage. Great question! Although, on the surface, my discussion with Jesus about sex appeared brief and limited, much deeper issues were addressed. This was possible because of two dynamics. First, any thought or question to Jesus, or High Guide or Amy, carries with it the context of all my experiences in life, of which they are fully aware.

Second, I often receive greater insight from their answers than is apparent from the words spoken.

Trey and I agree that before May of 1996 we shared a healthy sexual relationship. Yet, despite my love for my husband and my comfort sharing myself with him, I still possessed a deeply rooted sense of shame with sex. I originally attached shame and dirtiness to sex because of my biological father's numerous adulterous affairs. And then during my puberty, my parents addressed sex only from a biological or physical perspective. I don't remember being told about the tremendous love, goodness, and beauty attributable to sex with the right person. Sex was a "hush-hush" topic, which to me meant that it possessed an indecent quality, as did many of the other unspeakable topics. So my original negative association with sex was reinforced by the lack of mature and honest communication about it. It was also reinforced by the Catholic church's equation that premarital sex, not to mention other forms of sex, was sinful.

At the age of thirty-five and within a loving relationship, I still carried an element of the negativity that I had attached to sex during my adolescence. I now wished to remove this negativity, and Jesus removed it, both with the words He spoke and the insight He gave me. Yet He was not answering in a vacuum, but in the context of my loving, committed, mutually respectful relationship. He was telling me to let go of any and all shame that I attached to sex in my relationship with Trey and to accept and enjoy the beauty of our physical union.

Jesus was also telling me that our sexuality is a beautiful gift of God, a gift that should be celebrated, not denied. As with any act, the beauty springs from the intent of the heart. When we give of ourselves to another from love, then we experience God's highest desire for us. When we give because we are seeking power over another or because of the lack of our own power, the beauty is not realized. Now, every time I make love with my husband, I invite God to join us and His beauty to fill us. I no longer hide in shame.

Acknowledging Fear

After making love that Friday evening, Trey and I coexisted at a high that we had never reached before, in every aspect of our relationship: spiritual, emotional, mental, and physical. We were bathing in an ocean of God's love and blessings. We were engulfed in the beauty.

And then, in a moment, with one inadvertent comment, we were drowning. I blurted out the image I had received of our son. I spoke without thought or intent, as if I were compelled, just as when I told the psychic about the pink, nonexistent sunset. I was sickened that I had spoken of it. Since I was the one who received the image, I sensed that eventually I would understand it but that Trey did not have the means to resolve it. I felt insensitive for dumping this on him.

Trey's eyes were empty, revealing his shock and pain. I desperately wanted to help him, so I searched for possible explanations. In that process, I acknowledged a fear concerning our son that would surface in my conscious mind from time to time, but that I would immediately bury in my subconscious. I now feel that my guides compelled me to tell Trey so that I would see his distress, in turn urging me to deal with this issue. Otherwise, I might have continued to deny this image and my fear.

Before I address my fear with my son, I think it is important to provide a sense of my relationship with him. I had a strong bond with both of our children, but at that time our daughter was closer to Trey and our son was closer to me. As any mother would, I cherished the mutual affection and closeness that we shared. Trey often said that my son and I possessed a soul connection that you can't create; it's either there or not. I felt an intimate spiritual alignment with our son, enabling me to be particularly in tune with him.

Now for the first time, I consciously acknowledged the following: After the kids were asleep each night and right before I went to bed, I'd kiss our sleeping daughter goodnight, but I wouldn't enter our son's room to kiss him. I had rationalized my reluctance on the basis that he was a lighter sleeper, but that wasn't the real reason. I sensed something negative around him as he slept. It frightened me, and I didn't want to confront it. Within the shadow of my subconscious and conscious mind, I had interpreted that negative to mean that we might lose our son by death, before our deaths.

I would not normally share a thought like this, not knowing whether it was contrived or real. But this week was not a normal week, especially this day. And receiving an image of my child killing himself definitely was not normal. I now realized that in the past I had refused to acknowledge this feeling, which was one of heaviness and dread, because I feared confronting our son's death. I also realized that had I stopped running *from* the feeling and instead run *to* it, I could have investigated its origin and understood it far better. But I had allowed fear to have a greater power over me. So great, in fact, that even when I sensed we might lose our son, I refused to go into his room as he slept and take in every ounce of his being.

So I searched. Maybe this image was symbolic rather than literal. Because we had allowed our daughter to be more overbearing than was healthy, our son found it easier to let her will, her likes and dislikes, and her thoughts govern. He didn't have to think or "be" when his sister was willing and essentially demanding to do it for him. He was strangling and choking out his own self, his own identity, his own being and essence. The issue was not the physical death of our son in the future, as we were risking losing our son *now* in life.

I felt almost sure that the death of our son's essence was the meaning of the vision I had seen, but of course I wanted certainty and closure. I asked High Guide if I had in fact discovered the relevance of the image. His answer was that neither his nor my purpose was to predict the future. This was not the absolute assurance that I wanted, but it served a purpose. Trey and I continued to evaluate our son's situation, and, in the process, *we* discovered the true dynamic of our children's interaction as well as the solutions to help them.

This process deserves highlighting. The spiritual world rarely gives us complete answers because we gain greater understanding through self-discovery. As we pull together and grasp each piece of the truth in search of the whole truth, we intrinsically comprehend the reality of the situation. Say you have a math problem that is difficult to solve. You could ask a classmate for the answer, but then you still wouldn't understand the problem. Only when you work through the problem to find the answer do you truly understand it. Although it might be easier for God and His spirits to give us the answers we seek, we are benefited far more by their assistance in uncovering the answers ourselves.

I want to emphasize to our family and friends that Trey and I are now completely certain that this vision was symbolic in nature rather than literal. The vision served its purpose by prompting us to alter our parenting to address the problem. We have marveled over our son's blossoming since that day. Only a few weeks later, he was a more independent and expressive soul, starting his journey of self-discovery. Also, our daughter began to learn how to listen to others and respect their opinions. Just as God dramatically acted in my life to let me know it was time to get on with my spiritual journey, He alarmed me with this image, like a slap in the face, to wake me up so that we could address the issue before too much time had passed. And now, thankfully, Trey and I are fully aware of the issue, enabling us to deal with it appropriately whenever it arises.

This exercise was enlightening in another way. I now know that when I sense a negative or a fear, I should confront it. By denying it, the fear may come to fruition (as can happen with people who sense a health problem, such as cancer or heart disease, but are fearful of confronting it and so allow too much time to pass before helping themselves). Fear is a mental parallel to physical pain, in that both indicate that something is wrong. *Fear is a red flag to stop and investigate.* When we face our fears, we create the opportunity to right a wrong or unhealthy situation, to heal, to preclude something negative or harmful. I've flipped the fear coin in my life from tails to heads. I no longer tuck my tail and hide when I sense fear or danger; instead I attempt to address it head on.

Most of us have fears or thoughts of danger that enter our minds. Some of those fears are real and some are not. The trick is in determining which fears we should take seriously. My fear about our son was consistent and recurred from time to time for more than a year, even though I would set it aside. I now know that repetition of the fear was an indication that it was legitimate and not just imagined or created through normal motherly worries for my child.

As a final note, I want to suggest that there are different types of fear. The fear I am talking about here is a physical fear: the fear of harm, danger, or evil to body or soul. This physical fear is a warning signal that arises from our soul's intuition in order to help protect ourselves or another. We each inherently possess an intuitive fountain of wisdom, which, when we learn to trust it, can unleash powerful insight in our lives.

God's Gift

The kids returned from kids' night out bringing gifts of art work for Mother's Day. They had enjoyed their evening and were eager to share their creations. When I saw our daughter's art, I realized that she had also tapped into the spiritual energy surrounding us. She had drawn an angel, peering out from behind a cloud. She explained that the angel was watching over her from Heaven. Her picture also included a drawing of herself directly under the sun, with a light ray beaming down and touching the top of her head. Next to her was a larger-than-life flower. She drew a path of tic-tac-toe x's ascending from herself to this flower, which seemed to capture the blossoming of her spirit. I was awestruck to see that our four-year-old daughter, who was not aware of the happenings of this week and who had never drawn images like these before, was receiving the inspiration of God. I also sensed that our son was receiving the spiritual gift, as he was overflowing with positive energy, although he was too young to articulate his experience with us.

As I sat on the stairs examining this picture, our daughter sat on the couch with a quiet and pensive air. Trey sat next to her and asked if there was something she wanted to share with us. Her only response was, "God's gift." He was surprised by her choice of words, as she had never spoken in such terms. Trey said she seemed befuddled after responding that way and then nestled her head into his side for reassurance. Trey and I knew that she was receiving the right message but just didn't fully understand what it meant. Beautiful!

Although this day started climactically, the quieter moments in the presence of God, like this one with our children, did not go unnoticed. I cherish those moments of awareness when I am in that open place in my heart that enables me to recognize that God is speaking to me through nature, animals, or people, even though it is not outwardly apparent to anyone but me. They are subtle, personal moments of knowing and grace. They are around us all of the time, but we are quiet so little of the time that they often go unrecognized. But for some reason, seemingly by chance, we suddenly see God—in a sunset, a kitten, a friend, our child.

Today, I had other moments like this one with God, when God spoke softly to me through flowers. I realized that God was using the imagery of blossoming to capture the transformation in my family. Our earthly selves were merely the outer petals of a flower bud, encasing the majesty and the sweetness and the bloom inside. As our buds opened, the outer petals unfolded to reveal the beauty within, our soul. We were blossoming beyond our limited earthly selves, into an awareness of our broader, unlimited spiritual selves.

SEVEN

Revelations

day seven

Saturday, May 11, 1996

Saturday was the seventh and final day of my spiritual journey of a lifetime. It was also the first of several revelation days and, in that respect, the first day of school for my spiritual education. I feel it will be beneficial to illustrate the process from which these revelations were derived, so I've included several excerpts from my Saturday notes.

These revelations were partially channeled. I would begin a thought, idea, or question, and Amy would then take control of my hand and guide my writing to completion. As she answered and revealed, I received a supernatural awareness of the truth of the message. The truth felt like a wave of warm energy flowing through me that carried a sense of completion or wholeness. Even though I knew when we had captured the essence of a concept, in some cases I didn't understand the full significance or impact of the revelation. That understanding would evolve with time and experience. In the following excerpts, I've underlined Amy's guided writing to distinguish it from my writing.

1. The first revelation was revealed in my struggle to understand why *I* had been chosen for this incredible experience. Amy's answer was simply, "I am love." Understandably, this was quite a leap for me to grasp, having not even allowed myself to feel completely the love in my life. This truth was foreign yet awesome to discover. I now knew that the essence of every soul is love. We are one, we are the same, we are God's love.

> Said same basic prayer for years + God/Jesus has answered all of them this week ... b/4 my eyes + in my life + consciousness. That is pure love for me. Yet I'm struggling with "who am I?" to get this incomprehensible unbelievable gift
>
> *I am love*
>
> Amy helped me with that message + this one too. *Only you can discover life's secrets for yourself. You are doing well + will do better soon + better soon*
>
> We all are love — we're pure love blocked by negative energy
>
> *You are right. And there's more to learn. Much more*
>
> At first (yesterday) felt like an antennae — a very lucky antennae (sp) — but chose me b/c good receiver. Now feel more like my hindrance was not feeling worthy of love but ~~to do what~~ we all are love that must be acknowledged + nurtured + cherished + respected. Love — pure

I find it interesting that the phrase "I am love" is written in the middle of circles previously drawn on the notepad by our son. He drew circles on several other pages, and I noticed after my writing that many revelations were positioned in the center of those circles, most commonly personal revelations concerning my family.

Amy told me that I (we all) must discover life's secrets for myself (ourselves). When I wrote that we all are pure love blocked by negative energy, she answered, "You are right. And there's more to learn. Much more." Shortly after this she wrote, "that's what we all are love that must be acknowledged and nurtured and cherished and respected. Love—pure."

2. I then began to understand that I was chosen not because I was such a great "receiver," but because my great lesson in life was to feel love and know that I am love. Amy indicated that through my journey to discover love, "they will use me to help teach others about love."

So my last barrier was not feeling love - my great lesson which is why they will use me to help teach others about love

Yet I still have more, much more to learn about love + to allow permit myself to feel it more. A little overwhelming to think of feeling pure love on earth all the time.

I was always much more aware + felt guilty of not feeling love for someone then feeling love for all. There are many that I feel pure love for. And since Craig's birth I have sent that message to friends altho awkward

Why should loving feel awkward? Again your own limitations

Celestine Prophecy only book read connected to spiritual & I felt very connected to it, esp pact about sending your positive (now know love) energy to others + letting them shine which you would think diminishes you but makes you brighter, even brilliant

Maybe if accept that we are love all rest falls into place

I acknowledged that typically I didn't focus on feeling love for all people, but that I was very aware of, and felt guilty about, my lack of love for certain people. I also acknowledged that since Craig's death, I had told my close friends that I loved them despite the awkwardness of sharing that message. Amy responded, "Why should loving feel awkward? Again your own limitations." And when I talked about the message of *Celestine Prophecy* to send your positive energy, that is, love, to others, allowing them to shine, I acknowledged that one might think that giving away your positive energy would diminish your energy. But according to Amy it "makes you brighter, even brilliant." Amy further revealed that if we accept "that we are love all rest falls into place."

3. As a final universal revelation for the day, Amy gave me a sense of the purpose of each soul's journey in life. For me, it's helpful to look at our soul as a circle encompassing all of who and what we are, both positive and negative. As we fill our soul with more love/positive, less space is filled with negative. We effectively push out and remove the negative as we direct our lives along a path of love. So we are given a lifetime, or maybe several lifetimes, to accomplish this filling of our soul with love and goodness. Our purpose in living earthly lives is to become pure love, which is in fact every soul's ultimate destiny. Once we become pure love

So when Jesus forgave me I was pure love while I was with him. And love will remain the brightest light w/in me + only grow more brilliant. Our journey as spirits is to be pure in love on our own journey/work
  + then we will be pure light

Our paths as spirits/souls is to bring more + more love into our souls until we are pure love + then we will be pure light
We must do on own, with guidance, but we are in control + make the decisions. We control where we're going. We must face the obstacles for growth to occur — not deny them, suppress them or create own realities.

through our own choices and free will, we are then pure light, the light of Heaven, where we may then remain, that is, not return to earth, if we choose.

This is it—the root, the heart, the essence of our existence! I feel there is nothing greater to conceptualize, to share, than this simple climactic, spiritual truth: *WE ARE LOVE JOURNEYING TO BE PURE LOVE.* My body is trembling and energized by the sheer beauty of this knowledge.

The "love" that Amy and I refer to is more comprehensive than our typical conceptualization of love, for it is the love of God, the love that is God. God's love is an all-inclusive term for all positive qualities and emotions: love as we think of it in relationships, goodness, compassion and empathy, selflessness and kindness and service to others, peace and joy and harmony, patience and gentleness, appreciation and gratitude, mercy and forgiveness, and honesty and truth and integrity.

Several personal insights also came to light this day, one of which I'd like to share. Having been with Jesus in a profound face-to-face encounter, in addition to having the ability to mentally converse with my two guides, I felt that I presently had sufficient tools to accomplish God's purpose for me. I was comfortable with proceeding "as is," and I even stated my feeling to Trey.

Before going to bed, I went to High Guide for more fine tuning and conversation. He immediately brought me to a "higher" place where I sensed the presence of another, my brother Craig. Craig was different from the person I knew in life, yet I knew it was he. Craig told me that I had a lot more to learn and that I needed to work with my guides. High Guide and Craig had made it clear to me that I would learn much more about God and His world and that my connection with my guides would further evolve.

Craig left, and then I felt High Guide's energy enter my body for the first time. I could feel him breathing for, or maybe with, me. This merging of our energies felt odd, and might have been frightening or overwhelming had Craig not just advised me to expect the unexpected, in effect. Although I had no idea where we were going, I just opened up to be led by High Guide. I now know that this was our first "physical" connection, the first step in our work to allow High Guide to use my body to communicate with Trey and possibly others. And so day seven ended.

In Closing

I first learned that I was to write this book through an awareness given to me by the spiritual realm. They even gave me a title: "My Spiritual Journey of a Lifetime in One Week." Although ultimately I modified the title, I appreciated the message they sent me through it. Had they not included "one week," I would have struggled with choosing the day on which my spiritual experience ended. Day six would have been my natural choice, as it was the day I stood before Christ, the common ending to our lifetimes. I also felt that day seven was a day not too distinct from the several days following it. However, over time, I began to understand the spiritual realm's reasoning for including it.

In my mind now, standing before Jesus on day six was the climax, and day seven was the resolution, providing finality and closure to this experience, as I learned that I had been set on a path for my spiritual education. I knew that I had more spiritual truths to learn and, more important, to live and experience. God wanted me to be a messenger for Him, but before I could be a teacher, I must be a student, educated not by a book but by life. So in effect, Craig's message, to open up to the teachings of God's world, closed the door to this week's journey and opened the door to my spiritual journey going forward.

So here it is, summarily presented, my week-long spiritual journey of a lifetime:

Day 1, Sunday—I saw an aura, which I felt was the first solid evidence of my spiritual connectedness.

Day 2, Monday—I felt drawn to my guide through my dream, where I met Amy; my dream prompted me to buy a channeling book; when I started reading the book, I initially felt connected to channeling; upon further reading, I felt uncomfortable with the idea of a spirit entering my body to communicate with others.

Day 3, Tuesday—I listened to my heart and acknowledged that despite my uneasiness, channeling was my path; I made a commitment to channeling and began the channeling exercises.

Day 4, Wednesday—I received an affirmation of a spiritual or universal energy beyond myself when the energy force, "the hands," moved my head during a channeling exercise.

Day 5, Thursday—I connected with a spirit guide who talked to me in my head and then through my mouth during meditation; I recognized my block to feeling love through my friend's discussion of her inability to feel sadness; while praying, I was pulled into channeling where I met my two guides, learned about their purpose for me, and became familiar with their respective energies, and where I also was brought within the presence of God and Jesus and had a brief but moving encounter with Jesus.

Day 6, Friday—Trey and I experienced the blossoming of our spiritual relationship and our awareness that God had a purpose for us; I reached the "summit" of my week's experiences in my rebirth with Jesus through a cleansing face-to-face encounter; then I saw the beauty of the birth and blossoming of each member of my family, and I was given spiritual eyes or insight.

Day 7, Saturday—My spiritual education began through the revelations that I channeled; I received the important message that I was just at the beginning of my spiritual journey and that I had a lot more to learn before I would be ready to share my experience and any resulting spiritual insights.

I am often asked if I'm still having spiritual experiences. That question is tricky because it depends on one's outlook with respect to the word "experience." I look back at those seven days as a "spiritual experience" for two reasons. First, my encounter with the Divine was serendipitous in that I wasn't looking for it and this great thing just happened. And second, I didn't have any background in, knowledge of, or foundation for this level of spiritual connectedness, so I couldn't lead it, direct it, or cause anything to happen. I had no expectations, goals, or purposes. I was wholly a passenger, willing to go for the ride on this magnificent journey. So even though I still channel my guides and, since that initial week, have directly communicated with God and Jesus, these events no longer feel like spiritual experiences as I defined them because they occur as a result of my giving my life to God and allowing Him to act in my life in His supernatural ways. My continuing interactions with God's world, although incredible in the view of some people, are now normal, anticipated, and frequent events in my life.

I have followed High Guide's guidance with channeling so that now our communications are different in form than when we first established our connection. For the most part, I am no longer able to talk with High Guide and Amy in my mind at any time or to channel through writing. High Guide now uses my body to converse with Trey. Before we begin a channeling session, Trey and I will discuss the topics that we wish to address with my guides. I will then go into a meditative state where I invite High Guide's energy to enter my body and to use it to orally communicate. I am a vehicle for Trey and High Guide's conversations about life, God, and evolution, although I can mentally converse with High Guide and relay messages to Trey through High Guide.

I am now aware that my spirituality, not my humanness, is my fundamental essence. I am now aware that as love journeying to be pure love, only I direct the progression of my journey, through the choices I make, one of which is to follow God's guiding hand. I am now aware that I possess an inherent ability, as everyone does, to discover God's truth and to know God more richly, more intimately, than I ever knew was possible. It is through the God in me that I know these things. And it is through my week of spiritual awakening that I know, with absolute certainty, that anything and everything is possible—miracles are possible, if we eliminate the limitations within ourselves.

Many of our friends were curious to know if we were now preaching God! and Jesus! to all we meet and quoting the Bible and cleaning up our vices and . . . you get the picture. But the intriguing part is that we are not. Trey and I are the same individuals that we were before the week of May 5, 1996, except for one dramatic difference. Our spiritual base has evolved and been awakened to a place that can best be summarized by the words of French theologian and philosopher Pierre Teilhard de Chardin:

> We are not human beings having a spiritual experience. We are spiritual beings having a human experience.

And as much as I dislike the pompous air that "awakened" carries, it is the best word available to describe my new frame of reference: one lifetime of blindly meandering is over, and another lifetime of spiritual awareness, direction, and purpose has begun. Now I always carry with me a sense of God's purpose in life, a sense of the continuing evolution of each individual soul, and the knowledge that love, that is, God's energy, is the universal energy that bonds each soul to every other soul and to God. Love is the blood that flows through the arteries and veins of all of life; it is the bread and water that nourishes existence. Without love, we cannot thrive. I am a sponge saturated in the warm waters of gratitude, thankful that my pockets of emptiness, of fear, of unworthiness have been filled with the fruits of God's love.

I know that our growth with God not only is available to us all, but also is intended for us all. Your journey may not be even remotely similar to mine, as there are an infinite number of ways to spiritually connect with God and His world. Your connection will be personal to you, growing naturally in alignment with your belief system and your comfort.

Your experiences with God can occur anywhere along a spectrum of "directness": from indirect, such as maybe listening to your inner voice, or paying attention to coincidences in your life, or being aware of prayers that are answered or thoughts that are spiritually guided, or finding God's creative gift in you; to direct, such as encountering the Divine through dreams or visions, or healing others through the power of God's love, or developing psychic abilities, or perhaps channeling God's guides and teachers, as I have been given the ability to do.

You will sense or be drawn to your specific connection if you are willing, and if you pay attention to and trust your intuition. For instance, when I saw the psychic's aura, I felt no connection to auras, yet, for me, that experience affirmed the existence of something far grander, far more glorious, than my body could sense. That affirmation allowed me to find a path of connectedness totally different and unexpected.

Every step deeper into my journey, through each day, through the course of this week, I took mindfully. Of course, I had many nurturing nudges, some subtle and some not, from the spiritual realm, but the truth is that *my experience would not have occurred had I not been willing for it to happen.* I simply proceeded on faith. I would have loved to have had something solid at the outset to hold on to, to reassure me, something more than the intangible, the indefinable, the soft whisperings of the soul that can be so easily muted and drowned out. Still, I listened, quietly, tentatively, hopefully, and I accepted as real that which I could not see with my eyes or touch with my hands or wholly understand with my mind, but could only feel in my heart. Faith.

PART II

Lessons Learned

EIGHT

The Gift of Time and Experience

YEARS HAVE PASSED. ON THE SURFACE, many things seem the same in my life, but as I look back I recognize that powerful changes have occurred. Some have been subtle, many have not. Perhaps the most significant change has been in my perception of myself. I no longer view myself as a static and isolated being. I am an ongoing process, an evolving dynamic, a broadening energy; I am the expression of realizing, of quickening, of awakening. And in my continuous change and evolution, I am in the midst of appreciating how all of life, all of God's creation, is connected. I not only understand that every person is connected to God at every moment, but I know that each of us is connected to every human in every culture, to every animal and plant, to the earth, and to all consciousness and life beyond this world, no matter what form it may take. I also understand that God's wish for us is not to be reactive to life, but rather to be creative in life. I am empowered by my partnership with God and by the recognition of the immense creative ability given to us by God. I am unleashing my spirit from the reign of my limited earthly perspective to the vision of God's perspective so that I can become all that God desires for me to be.

Over the first couple of years following our awakening, God presented Trey and me with many opportunities for change in our lives, and we seized them. Although wonderful changes, they were completely absorbing. The biggest change was the addition of our third (and final) child. She is a beautiful spirit. We honored our great soul-friend by choosing "Erin" as our daughter's middle name.

A month after our daughter was born, we were on a plane to Colorado to look at a job opportunity for Trey. We fell in love with a small, family-oriented community and decided to move. Although we were excited about starting our Colorado family adventure, Trey and I each left thirty-six years of Texas behind, our extended families, most of our friends, and the place we had always envisioned our future.

Our lives were "new" everything. A new baby in and of itself can be quite disruptive and time consuming. Maybe it is not such an ordeal after you have uprooted once before, but a new house, city, state, schools, job, friends, AND a new baby consumed me for a year. All earthly matters were in flux. And although nothing appeared solid, what really matters was solid: our love of God, our love of each other, and our desire to grow with God.

I now recognize the beauty that this time gave me. In addition to providing many external growth opportunities, the period after my experience also provided an important opportunity for internal growth. Although the catalyst of hot water turns tea leaves into tea immediately, the tea still requires time to steep for best flavor. Likewise, my experience was the catalyst for my internal growth, but only with the passage of time has my character begun to change to embody the essence of that experience. As an example, now instead of merely repeating the words of my guides, I can more fully appreciate their

The Gift of Time and Experience

truth and significance. I am better equipped and more confident to share what we have learned through our relationship with God.

As a result of the wondrous events of May 1996 and the "steeping" that has occurred since, my daily focus is in thoughts, feelings, and actions such as these:

- I wake up and go to bed with prayers to God. Through the course of the day, my thoughts turn to God often, and almost everything I think about now carries with it the context of God and love.
- I often see God acting in my life and in the lives of others. Even when I don't see Her work, I trust that God is acting, as Her presence and interactions in this world are ubiquitous.
- I frequently ask myself these questions: What can I learn from this particular situation? How can I improve myself? How can I help another? When I have a negative reaction to a person or a situation, I consider: What is my issue, or what is it that I need to see more clearly about myself?
- I remind myself to BE who I am. This is a little difficult to explain. I would find myself claiming that "this is who I am" or "this is what I believe." Now, rather than trying to convince others or even myself of those matters, I just live them; they are what I choose to be. The reality of who and what I am is realized only through who and what I choose to "be" in any moment anyway.
- I remember that I am love; be love.
- I strive to allow others to be—regardless of who they choose to be—without judging them.
- I try not to have my own expectations or agendas for doing God's work, and when I do, I try to recognize them and release them, so that I do not interfere with God working through me.
- As God has asked us to do, I turn my burdens over to Her.

- I try not to push onto others, or be overbearing with, my beliefs and experiences, but to open myself to be a natural and pure instrument of God's love.
- I pray from the heart and then release my prayers knowing that God will answer when and how it is best for me.
- I listen more to God and to others.
- I see purpose in many more, and much smaller, things.
- I see beauty in many more, and less obvious, aspects of life.
- I remind myself that every experience is spiritual no matter how seemingly inconsequential, that there are no coincidences, that change is the only constant, that I should enjoy the journey rather than worry about the outcome, and that it is possible to create Heaven here on earth.
- I am aware of my interconnection with all of life and that I affect life not only through my words and actions, but also through my thoughts. Intent alone is immensely creative.
- When I notice myself acting or thinking in a way that disappoints me, I change my action or thought the next moment.
- I still have both significant and petty issues in my life, but I now try to address them within the context of love.
- I still have pain, disappointments, and struggles in my life, but I also have a deeply rooted sense of peace knowing that God is always with me and that with God's help I will use these for the growth of my soul.
- I am truly happy to be alive, I appreciate the gift of opportunity in each day, I thrive on God's use of me to help others to grow with Her, and I continue to deconstruct my wall to feeling love.

Although I admit that the magnitude of learning ahead of me is as awesome as what I have learned so far, I cherish this opportunity to present God's truth, wisdom, joy, beauty, and love as Trey and I have discovered it, or maybe more accurately, remembered what our souls already knew. There is so much I yearn to share.

NINE

Perspective Now

AFTER MY BROTHER DIED, I appreciated for the first time the fragility of life. When my children were born, I loved them in a way that I had never loved another. There are moments in life that change us in unexpected and indelible ways. They are the experiences that shake us up, shift our perspective, or crack the foundation that we stood on. We are left to realign, redefine, or rebuild ourselves over time. My spiritual experience was one of those moments. I did not know exactly where it would lead me or how I would be different, but I had no doubt that profound changes were coming.

Time has ticked away, and my new spiritual foundation has settled. As I seek to capture my paradigm shift, I recognize that my change in perspective has been far greater than I anticipated. Although the things I share may be viewed as controversial by some, the best I can do is honestly convey what I have come to know. There is an immense amount of material, and some of it is very dense, so I have broken it down into bullet points to give the reader obvious places to rest and reflect before reading on. Here are the principles that have resonated as truth in my experience of God:

- We are *spiritual* beings having human experiences, as quoted earlier from Teilhard de Chardin. We are beings of spirit that have existed since the beginning of creation and will exist for all of eternity. The essence of our spirits is the energy of God, which is simply love. Although our spirits understand this, our minds may not, presenting disharmony and unfulfillment in our lives. When we remember that we are from God, of God, and with God always, we begin to understand our purpose and place in this life and in our eternal existence. Reconnecting to our true essence, our spirits, brings us peace by bringing us home.

- We are spiritual beings having *human* experiences. Our spirits take on physical, bodily form on the physical, earth plane so that we can "experience" or "live" our beingness and, accordingly, grow and evolve. Just as a child rarely learns lessons by accepting a parent's experiences but must learn through his or her own experiences, as the children of God we require the human, physical existence to experience ourselves. Our journey on earth is the opportunity God gives us (and we give ourselves) to define who and what we are. When our spirits choose to take on physical form, the inherent limitations of a three-dimensional, physical environment can trick us. The world is flat, until we recognize the illusion. We are our minds and bodies, until we realize that we are spirit.

- We are spiritual beings having human *experiences*. We change and grow and evolve with each experience, constantly redefining who we are. The personal experience is the driving force in our evolution. As a teenager, I became aware that my actions defined me, shaped me, but that was only the beginning of this life's journey. I did not yet know who I wanted to be. Now I not only know who and what I desire to be, but I also understand that the power to get me there is within me. I can create any Jenice I wish to. In fact, I recreate who I am from moment to moment by the choices I make. While we are on earth, we are in the game. The earthly plane is the playing field where experiences both good and bad constantly confront us. Each of us individually must choose whether to be an active player or a passive pawn in the game of life.

- The simple purpose of life is the evolution of our souls to eventually become pure love and at one with God. The path and momentum of this journey are determined by our choices. Spiritual awakening means becoming aware of both this purpose and how the laws of the universe operate to help us achieve our ultimate evolution. Yet even before our awakening, we are headed down the same path, we're just not cognizant of it.

- For most souls, the journey to pure love is long and laborious, requiring numerous lifetimes to achieve. We are reincarnated not for the sole purpose of continuing our existence, for we have always existed and will always exist. Each earthly experience continues and furthers our evolution. We are reborn a changed soul, further evolved by our prior lives and experiences. When we are in the spiritual realm between lives, we are able to see the summation of our past experiences and accordingly choose the circumstances of our next lifetime that will best address the areas where we need to grow.

- We choose diverse lives to round out our experiences, learn different lessons, and further evolve. One life may be a Christian experience, another Buddhist, another Jewish. From each great religion and each great leader or master, we can learn great things. One life may be as a Caucasian, another African-American, another Chinese. One life may be rich in material possessions and another poor. From each chosen life and chosen struggles, we are presented with different opportunities for growth. This makes so much sense. As a spiritual person who believes that Jesus is God's highest love expressed and thus the way to God, I now can hold that belief and still accept that every soul has the freedom and the right to choose the human experience necessary for his or her own evolution. God, and Jesus as the son of God, allow us this choice. Imagine the consequence if we could collectively broaden our awareness to understand this. We would eliminate much of the prejudice, hatred, and fear in our world and raise our consciousness to the higher energies of love, acceptance, and peace.

- Inherent in this ongoing evolutionary process is the fact that we will never be faced with a last-chance, lost-cause scenario. Messing up in this life is not fatal. One soul may learn a lesson after only one mistake, while another may need one hundred mistakes to learn the same lesson. Although there may be a significant event or life-defining moment that a soul fails to respond to in line with its highest purpose, that experience accumulates with that soul's other experiences. Eventually, maybe in this life, maybe in a subsequent life, that soul will learn the lesson and grow. Each experience is what that soul needs. Extrapolating this process further, it becomes clear that no person is better than another or inherently different from another; we are merely at different stages of evolution.

- The ultimate law of the universe is that you reap what you sow. This is known as karma in spiritual terminology. *Everything* you give out to the universe flows back to you, both positive and negative. Many of us have a sense of this but limit this principle in a couple of ways. One limitation is our assumption of a direct correlation. The universal law of cause and effect does not mean that when we give our love to someone, that person will necessarily love us back. It does mean that we will receive love in the whole of our experience. We also tend to confine karma to this lifetime. We believe that upon death, we will be judged by the Source or Creator, God, and that this judgment determines our final resting place or status. In reality, the karma or effects we create are carried with us through our journey both in and out of our physical manifestations.

The corollary to karma is "like attracts like." If we are dishonest, we attract dishonest people. If we are loving, we attract love. If we are prejudiced in this lifetime, we will be the victim of prejudice at another time, whether in this lifetime or another one. When we are generous, abundance comes our way. Once we have a solid understanding of karma, we are able to see that God does not sit and wait to judge, but rather has set up the mechanics of the universe to autonomously apply the principle of cause and effect. God has shown us the truth through Jesus and other masters. God created the universe to respond to us in accordance with our own choices. Choices that bring love and truth into our lives result in harmony. Choices that oppose love and truth bring us disharmony so that we will recognize how our choices have distanced us from God. Thus, through the choices we make, we each create the quality of our own existence in both the earthly realm and the spiritual realm. Effectively, we are our own teachers and judge, with God's karma implementing the lessons. Karma is represented by Jesus' golden rule to do unto others as you wish others to do unto you.

❧ The beauty and grace in our journey is that every soul is destined to evolve to pure love. We are not limited by time or a specific number of lifetimes or even by blindness to our journey. And no matter in what plane or realm we presently reside, whether it be earth, Heaven, purgatory, limbo, hell, or any other plane that may exist, we are working on our evolution.

Furthermore, we are never alone in our work. The God energy or spirit is always with us, as are Her helpers. I fondly call God's helpers "love spirits," as they are entities of God's love and light. These love spirits include guides, teachers, and angels that are spiritually connected to us. Some of our loved ones whose physical deaths have preceded ours are also with us, those who are at a stage in their evolution that enables them to help others. And we each have a "soul circle" that not only helps us to grow, but grows itself with our growth. Our soul circle is a group of souls who are at a level of evolution similar to that of our own soul. Many of these souls have shared other lifetimes with us in varied relationships. Our "pep squads" in the spiritual realm are constantly guiding us to experiences we need in this lifetime. It is obvious from my spiritual week that my brother Craig is working to help me.

Knowing that our evolution is continuous and not finally determined by this life, we can understand that Heaven is not a final resting place, or a fishing hole for fishermen, or a snow-covered mountain for skiers, although fishing and skiing are experiences possibly available to us there. (I believe that at a certain stage in our evolution it is possible for us to create our Heavenly experiences, as depicted in the movie *What Dreams May Come*.) Rather, Heaven is a realm of love and peace to which we return to heal our soul so that we may continue our journey to pure love and aid other souls in their journey.

- Hell as *eternal* punishment and condemnation does not exist. However, there is a realm seemingly "without God" where spirits exist who have refused to choose God's light and love.

Although this realm may be effectively hell, it is not eternal, as every soul has the option of choosing God, choosing love. God will never turn away a soul that chooses love. Redemption is always possible and desired by God. Although by appearances hell is a realm without God, in reality, God is even there, for we cannot exist without God, as God is All That Is. Yet God allows us all to make our own choices, including a choice to deny Him and His existence. Hell is the realm of the decision to deny God.

- Evil is real, but it is a choice. Evil is not an all-powerful force that can take you unwillingly. At the spiritual level, evil is always disempowered by good, by God's love. An exception to this choice pertains to souls incarnated on earth who are afflicted with severe mental illness and do not have the strength of clarity to ward off evil.

- Sin is a choice against or away from love and our soul's highest interests. Many of us are taught that we sin when we hurt others. Although true, this conceptualization does not capture the core of sin. When we hurt others, the sin lies in the wrongdoing to our own soul. We also sin strictly by hurting ourselves, without hurting another. Since my spiritual awakening, I dislike using the word "sin" because of the connotation I attached to it from my Catholic upbringing. Sin does not possess the gravity or permanence that I once believed it did, and it is not defined by seemingly random, absolute rules such as those prohibiting premarital sex, cohabitation, dancing, or drinking caffeine. Sin is merely a convenient word that describes a personal choice that negatively affects a soul's evolution. In Chapter Fifteen, I address sin, and forgiveness of sin, in greater detail.

- Love and honesty are the cornerstones and conduits for our evolution. Love is the highest energy and encompasses each and every positive emotion and characteristic. Love is the ultimate, final choice and destination for us all. Honesty is one of love's numerous derivations. Our own dishonesty with ourselves or others, as well as others' dishonesty with us, creates a fog that disorients us. We expend valuable time and energy lost and confused and find ourselves on dead-end paths. Honesty is the light that is capable of penetrating the fog and illuminating our highest paths. Our honesty exemplifies not only our respect, but also our love, for ourselves and others. Our state of awareness depends on honesty, for the truth is the truth, the truth "is." We do not alter the truth with our denial of it or our inability to see it clearly. When we unveil the truth through honesty, we become self-aware and our souls experience a harmony with the truth. We gain strength and clarity and lose our fear. Self-awareness, including spiritual awareness, leads us more directly down our evolutionary path.

- No matter our age, we are all children in the context of our earthly experiences:
  - Children learn through *self* discovery and experience.
  - Children are dependent on adults as we are dependent on God. I am referring not to our survival but to the ability of our souls to grow and thrive. We need God's assistance to evolve.
  - As children cannot fully grasp many aspects of life until they age and mature, we cannot fully understand the full scheme of God and our spiritual path while on earth. For example, children do not understand sexual relations. When they become curious, we feed them small pieces of the bigger picture in terms they can understand. God does the same for us by giving us pieces of the bigger picture in terms we can grasp. But our earthly, three-dimensional experience is inherently limited, precluding us from seeing and understanding the complete picture.

I understand this limiting aspect of our earthly experience when I contemplate the circumstance of standing before Jesus. My physical body was in a bathroom in my home, yet my spirit was in another realm. If Trey had walked in, he would have seen me, but not Jesus. Yet I was with Jesus, seeing Him with my own eyes. Our essence, our existence, and our purpose far exceed the scope that our five earthly senses afford us. And still, with the knowledge that our Creator is unconditionally loving, we are able to trust in God that which we are unable to comprehend.

- God gives us free will . . . yet God acts in history for a purpose. I discuss these two principles in Chapter Fourteen.
- With every birth of a life on this earth, there will be a death, and in every life, there will be both beauty and pain. Yet it is the pain, the struggles, the tragedies that cause some of us to deny and reject our loving God. How can God be when there is so much suffering in the world? Remembering that we are childlike in our ability, or rather our inability, to wholly understand the dynamics of our environment, consider that some of the "bad things" that occur in our life are accidental and random, some occur by virtue of the free will and choice of another or ourself, and some are even purposeful, that is, struggles agreed to before birth to serve a higher purpose of God. I am *not* suggesting that we should seek bad events or obstacles, nor should we justify our own "bad" actions with this awareness. What we can do with this awareness is take the blame away from God. We can also open our hearts to understand that when we suffer, God experiences our pain. When we blame or reject God, we deny ourselves some of God's greatest and most precious gifts, those of comfort, peace, strength, and the rest of Her miraculous healing graces.

By fully appreciating that the bad comes with the good in our earthly experience, we depersonalize the bad events in our lives. We recognize that in our painful experiences, God is not targeting us or punishing us or abandoning us. From a spiritual perspective, nothing happens against the will of our soul. By virtue of choosing the earthly experience, we have agreed to the whole of the experience, both good and bad, and both random and purposeful. There is also much pain in life that we tend to view as random, when in reality we collectively have chosen or allowed it to happen. A couple of examples are poverty and starvation, which exist because of our collective choice and tendency to hoard rather than to give.

When we broaden the way we view the struggles in our lives, we begin to see the opportunities presented for growth as we are confronted with hardships, and that there is beauty even in strife. In many ways, confrontation forces us to awaken from our sleep. We are forced to dig deeper into ourselves to find strength, purpose, and self-worth.

I've shared my struggles of growing up in a dysfunctional home, the death of my brother, and the impending death of Erin, but I would like to share an additional struggle that was a tremendous learning experience for me. I flunked the third day of the state bar exam. To make matters worse, I was the first person at my law firm ever to flunk the bar. At twenty-five years of age, I had my first significant experience with failure. My initial response was humiliation, which drained my self-confidence. With Trey's help, I saw that I had two choices: I could allow the failure to defeat me or I could use it to broaden myself. I chose to grow. Had I chosen self-defeat, my environment would have allowed me to remain there.

That experience provided an opportunity for intense self-reflection and, ultimately, honesty with myself. Even though I felt overwhelmed by the magnitude of the failure, I was able to dig deep for confidence and strength and to acknowledge that the failure did not define me. I saw how I had set myself up for failure by creating an insurmountable obstacle and from that I learned that I must never allow fear to paralyze me and create a self-fulfilling prophecy as I had done. I also learned that failure is okay and even natural, as no one is successful at everything in life. Although my fear had created the monster that caused my failure, I did not allow my fear of the consequences of failure to stifle a positive and productive reaction. In the end, I found strength that I didn't know I possessed. No matter the cause, how we choose to respond to obstacles leads us down different paths of growth and defines us in different ways.

❧ Our greatest limitations are self-imposed. We restrict our potential and greatness by clinging to fear, by denying our inherent creative abilities, and by refusing to open the door to God's love for us and His desire and power to assist us. We fear the unknown, we fear failure, we fear isolation if we stray from the "norm," we are insecure, we possess low self-esteem and self-worth, and we convince ourselves that success and greatness are not intended for us. We fail to recognize authentic success and greatness and instead gauge our achievements in accordance with superficial and materialistic standards. We can truly be our own worst enemy.

Mother Teresa was a woman who lacked physical prowess and financial wealth. Yet her life exemplifies true greatness. Her tremendous accomplishments did not derive from her humanness or her physical, external manifestations. Her greatness derived from her internal essence or spirit. Through her example, we can begin to see that the spirit is without limitation or confinement unless we choose to self-impose those restrictions. Mother Teresa's wise words, "We do not do great things, but rather small things with great love," can help us to understand the power of love. To embark on our highest path and reach our highest purpose, we need to shed the chains of limitation and tap into our ability to create a better life for ourselves and others. The power is within and is truly unlimited.

- Organized religion is imbued with beauty and wisdom, yet it also imposes limitations of its own. I believe that when we are able to see the true nature of organized religion in both its positive and negative aspects, then we are better able to use its positive offerings to grow with God. The beauty is obvious. Organized religion is a wonderful forum for enhancing our relationship with God, as tremendous knowledge can be gained from people who have dedicated their lives to God and the study of the Bible or other holy texts. The limitations are more subtle. Many derive from the fear-based teachings of some religions, such as guilt, punishment and condemnation for our sins, our separation from God, and intolerance to differing beliefs and lifestyles, to name a few. Although the focus of organized religion is on a perfect God, limitations are inevitable because the organizers, leaders, and members of religion are imperfect human beings. As an example, it has always intrigued me that the behavior that religion deems as sinful changes over time, although we intuitively know that God's truth is unchanging and eternal. In Chapter Fifteen, I challenge the role that many of us have given to organized religion, and I offer a broader perspective of the purpose that it can serve in our lives.

- I no longer view my children as my possessions, *my* children, but instead I view them as God's children, whose spirits have been entrusted to Trey's and my care. This distinction is significant in the working dynamic between parent and child, at least it was for me. This may sound odd, but it hurt initially when I shifted my focus with respect to my kids. My emotional response was that they were mine and I didn't want them taken away from me. Yet this response helped me to see the element of ownership that I had in my children and the credit that I took from them.

As with each other awareness given to Trey and me by God, this one also has brought great beauty to our lives. My role as a mother transformed. I released my possessive bond with my children, and with that liberation our relationship broadened, allowing them and me to grow in ways much greater than were possible before. I freed myself because I no longer act with the purpose of "controlling" my children. I am no longer trying to force my will for them onto them. I freed my children through my recognition that they are independent souls making their own choices in life.

As parents, most of us strive to provide our children with well-balanced meals, but as new parents quickly realize, we can't force our children to eat what they don't want to eat. Yet we are acting responsibly by offering them good, healthy options. Similarly, our job as parents is to shower our children with all of our love, guidance, and insight, though limited and imperfect, and then let them shine and falter through their own decisions and experiences. No doubt they will make mistakes, just as we have done, as children and parents. I now appreciate that my children will learn many of their greatest lessons through their mistakes, just as I have learned through mine.

Although our children's choices may be different from ours, we honor and serve them by permitting them to personally choose their experiences. Of course, I am not talking about letting children do whatever they want without limits. I am talking about parenting with the understanding that our children are whole souls who have come to earth with an innate understanding of the lessons and growth that they need to evolve to greater love.

I see our ultimate goal as parents as helping our children to strive for their highest path and potential. We may think this is difficult, or even impossible, if we are not aware of our own highest purpose. But I have no doubt that this goal is attainable, because all that is required of us is that we empower our children—by building them up rather than tearing them down. When we give them our unconditional love and acknowledge their own power and greatness, we give them the tools to strive for their highest purpose: the tools of love, self-worth, security, confidence, and caring. If we look at all people, even our own children, as independent and whole spiritual beings born onto this earth with the purpose of choosing their own experiences for their soul's evolution, then we open the door for God's purpose, rather than our expectations, to flourish.

I believe that the matching of a soul to his or her parents is divinely governed. Whether karma dictates the selection or the soul decides, there is a spiritual purpose in the union. Coming to this realization has led to two interesting consequences in my life. First, I have taken away much of the blame I placed on my own parents for my dysfunctional childhood, knowing that I either chose them or needed them for my spiritual growth. Second, understanding that the individual spirits of my children have been brought to me by God's design, and through their choice, I now understand and appreciate the dynamic of our relationship as a spiritual partnership. I recognize that I will learn as much from them as they will learn from me. I have realigned my priorities from a primary focus on the worldly needs, such as room and board, physical and emotional safety, and academic teachings, though they are still important, to a primary focus of helping the children to know their spiritual essence and to tap into their authentic power.

Each child is unique, with his or her own needs and with an individualized path. Someone once pointed out to me that although I am a mother of three, I am the only mother for each of my children. I often reflect upon this wisdom to remind myself that I should not mother my children collectively, but rather individually. I do not view fairness as a same-and-equal-to-all concept. I view fairness to my children as stepping into the shoes of each of them, getting a glimpse of his or her world and perspective, and then responding in accordance with each child's needs. By viewing my relationship with each of my children as a unique and distinct spiritual partnership, I recognize the trust and faith that both God and my child have in me to support and nurture my child's soul. I often thank my children for choosing me as their mother, and I expressly promise them that I will do the best job I can for them.

- We strive for our highest purpose by focusing on our spiritual essence and then turning to God and allowing Her to direct and guide us. With every experience, we are confronted with choosing one path among numerous options. God is able to see the whole of the interactions in this world that we are not able to see. When we ask God to help us to see our highest purpose in any situation, we are asking Her to show us Her path of greatest insight, beauty, and consequence. Although I still pray for specific results that I desire, I "qualify" my requests by asking that God's will and highest purpose be served.

- When we give our will to God, we each have the same purpose: love of and service to God through love of and service to ourselves and others. We are simply serving as a window to God for others, or as a channel or instrument of God's love. Although we each have the same purpose, we implement that purpose in innumerable ways. I have found it interesting that interests and actions of mine that I once categorized as "earthly" because they were seemingly unrelated to God and His will for me, I now see as venues within which I can channel the energy and love of God. Everything that we do, career, play, and relationships, are all vehicles to experience and exemplify the magnificence of God. It is all about opening ourselves for God to act for us and through us.

These new seeds of knowledge have solidly rooted in my life and continue to grow and flourish with each and every day of experiencing life. Just as every garden requires attention and nourishment to thrive, I am mindful to nourish and feed my garden, my soul, by focusing on God and love and by choosing to open myself to a broader and more comprehensive understanding of God and Her workings.

TEN

Love

I AM BOTH AMAZED AND RELIEVED that much of the knowledge I have gained through my spiritual experience and my subsequent channeling of High Guide and Amy has been addressed and confirmed in the spiritual books that I have read since May of 1996. The ultimate, underlying truth and foundation of spirituality is that the essence of every soul is love, which is the energy and essence of God.

Love.

I am love.

God = love.

God = love = me.

The truth is incredibly elegant, incredibly simple. So simple in fact that even when we learn that we are love, we still may find it difficult to understand or accept. Surround yourself with love. Bathe in it. Visualize love as the center and core of your essence. Allow yourself to exude love from the inside out. Accept that each of us is created from a spark of God, and then imagine your spirit to be a star of God's love and light with the brilliance of this energy shining in all directions and touching all existence, everywhere. See that each of us is connected to everyone and everything through the penetrating touch of God's love and light. How fortunate we are that love is our answer, our truth, our purpose, our essence! How glorious our God that His gift of creation is founded upon the greatest of all things—LOVE!

The energy of the universe is love. The dynamic of the universe is set up to cultivate greater love. When we live a life of love, more love and beauty come our way, for we are within the natural flow and course of the universe. Our lives seem to fall into place. When we live life not choosing love, negatives come our way to help us recognize that we are not choosing love. We find ourselves at dead-ends, confronted with obstacles, and experiencing more pain than joy and beauty. These negative experiences are spiritual indicators that we are not on track with love. If we accept that we are love and live that truth, then, as Amy says, "All else will fall into place."

Many of us make a leap of faith in our belief in God without physical evidence, and eventually we have a relationship with God. We come to know within our hearts, our souls, that there truly is a God. Our belief evolves with time and faith. Make the leap now that all is love. Choose love to guide your every thought, word, and action. We evolve by loving others. Others evolve by our loving them.

When Jesus was being tested by the Pharisees, He was asked, "Teacher, which is the greatest commandment in the Law?" Jesus replied: "Love the Lord your God with all your heart and with all your soul and with all your mind. This is the first and greatest commandment. And the second is like it: 'Love your neighbor as yourself'" (Matthew 22:36-38). This is the most important "law" of God, and it ties many of the great religions together. Love of God, ourselves, and our neighbors is universal and encompasses all. Jesus was telling us that if we simply follow this greatest commandment, then we will naturally obey and keep all of God's other commandments. By being love and loving all spirits, we are acting in godly ways. Jesus defined our purpose with His answer. This truth is both our journey and our destination.

In order for me to begin to live this truth, I had to learn to love myself first. I needed to know and to accept my fundamental essence. Who am I to have had this ineffable experience? Amy's answer—I AM LOVE. Her response was truly a new revelation to me.

It is so obvious to me now why my experience was what it was. I felt unworthy of God's unconditional love. I embraced guilt because I was not perfect. Unworthiness and guilt were my barriers to love. And because I did not love myself wholly, I could not accept the full experience of love from God and others. God knew the exact experience that I needed at that point in my life to tear down my barriers to love. So He presented me with a cleansing experience that I identified with and valued as a result of my Catholic upbringing: one of confession, remorse or repentance, and then forgiveness. I was purely, wholly, completely bare to Jesus. I stood naked before God in body and soul, that is, physically, mentally, emotionally, and spiritually. Nothing was hidden. Every facet of my being was revealed to Jesus. And He forgave me. He made me pure. He revealed His mercy and His love for me. Because of my pure nakedness, there is no qualification or excuse or condition on which I can diminish God's love, forgiveness, and mercy. I cannot say that if Jesus had only seen this part of me, He wouldn't have forgiven me or He wouldn't love me. God knew that through this specific epiphany, I would both see my past denial of love and accept His unconditional love for me.

So I accepted that I am love, although that didn't mean that I automatically felt it. That feeling has evolved with my continuous focus on love. I often repeat "I am love" during meditation and prayer, as I have learned from the spiritual books I have read about the immense creative power of the "I am" statement. I also am fully aware of my imperfections. But instead of attaching guilt or unworthiness to them, I use my self-awareness to try to better myself. I am constantly growing and seeing realities and truths in my life that I was unable to see before. Through this growth, I now understand that I am love and that you are love and that my neighbor is love and that my enemy is love. This knowledge changes the way I look at everything and everyone.

No matter how foreign another person is to you or how differently others may lead their lives, they are love. Love eliminates prejudice, love eliminates hate, love eliminates fear. Love yields only greater love. I am not claiming to be a master of love because I am far from realizing such a lofty goal, but I have taken the first step by accepting that we all are love.

I am continually striving to act in loving ways, and that is a great thing. But I have recently learned two greater truths with respect to love. Both lessons were learned in connection with the "downfall" of a person I'm very close to. I will call this person "Carl." Carl recently lost both his job and his marriage because of his deceit and dishonesty. Although I do not respect or condone Carl's rejection of honesty, I still love him, as he is a part of my life and he is God's child and therefore love. I have witnessed, and experienced myself, the hurt and pain he has brought upon many people I care about, and I am angry with him for that. Yet he needs the love and support of his friends and family to help him get through this difficult time. And he has been given that love and support. The answer for Carl, which seems simplistic and obvious when you are not in it, is for him to examine what it is about himself that got him in this predicament and then to use this opportunity to change and grow. But so far he hasn't, and I'm afraid that he never will (in this life). That hurts. It hurts because I want him to know the love, happiness, and peace that is available to him. It hurts because those of us who love him find it difficult to hold on to peace ourselves when he has not learned the lesson of his struggle, which brings me to my first lesson learned.

For a time, I allowed myself to be pulled down by Carl's failure to take his higher path. High Guide helped me to rise from this negative place with the following advice during a channeling session: No matter how much love we give Carl, it is his choice to accept it or not. He has chosen not to. Accordingly, I should not allow myself to be negatively burdened by his choice. The point is not to stop loving him but to realize that we can only give love, not force others to accept it. A sad but enlightening lesson learned.

High Guide's message has a couple of layers of depth. The most apparent is that our act of giving is not always accompanied by acceptance. I am a perfect example of this. I was surrounded by the love of God, my husband, and others in my life, and yet I refused their gift.

From this layer, we can go deeper to extrapolate that we have control only over our own actions and intent and no control over others'. Although we accept this, we are conflicted when a loved one is in turmoil. Our hearts are so closely entwined with our loved ones that we suffer with them. Many of us allow ourselves to be pulled into the pit with a loved one. This is dangerous because we are relinquishing our control. If I allow Carl's choices to pull me into the pit, then I risk surrendering my personal power to Carl and becoming dependent on his choices to get me out of the pit. My frustration, lack of peace, and sense of helplessness do not benefit either Carl or me.

Our love is not exemplified by sinking with our loved ones. Our love is greatest when we are compassionate, strong, and whole in ourselves. So instead of giving Carl's choices power over me by allowing them to diminish my happiness and peace, I recognized that the most positive influence I have with Carl is through my interaction with, and response to, him: I share my love for him with him, and I pray for him. I pray that in this life he will remember that his essence is love, and I pray that he will choose love and honesty to guide him.

The second lesson learned was more personal to me. I realized that my anger over Carl hurting many people that I deeply care for made it difficult for me to show Carl my love for him. As I now seek to act in loving ways, I tried to treat him as I thought love would treat him. I guess I was trying to second guess how love would act, or, in other words, how I should respond to him if I was coming from love. Granted this was a loving response, but it was not love responding.

During a meditation, I was thinking about Carl and what I should do for him. Then the truth surfaced. Our purpose is not to think, speak, and act as we think love would think, speak, and act. *Our purpose is to love and then think, speak, and act.* Be love . . . think love . . . speak love . . . act love. Another one of those subtle yet extremely significant distinctions.

Even now I have to remind myself of what I already know: Carl is facing this obstacle and struggle in the manner he needs for his own evolution; and Carl is not a "lost cause," as his evolution will continue through other earthly experiences and in the spiritual realm. My desire for Carl's higher level of happiness will not supersede the experiences his soul needs and chooses now.

Through this discussion of Carl, it is obvious that I have reflected and focused on how I share my love with others, but you may be wondering whether I now feel love. I am pleased to share that *I am now a receiver of love*. These words embrace my most awesome achievement in life. Although I still have moments when I block the love, more often than not, I truly feel love. I accept and feel God's love for me. I accept and feel the love of my husband, my children, my family, and my friends. I experience the inherent interconnectedness of love even beyond myself. Trey and I often shed joyful tears over the overwhelming beauty and strength that we receive from the love in our lives and the love in the world. And I love myself. I have shed my armor of unworthiness that allowed me only to give love but not to receive it. I have replaced my armor of unworthiness with God's armor of love. With God's love, I feel as if I exist within a protected dome of peace, joy, and beauty. These qualities not only surround me but permeate my very core.

Of these qualities, the peace is the most powerful for me, far exceeding anything I could attain before my spiritual awakening. With the knowledge that I am love and am loved by God, my peace is indestructible. Of course that doesn't mean that I cannot, or will not, feel pain, because I do. I guess it is a matter of relativity. Because I now view all events within God's grander spiritual plan, I have a handle on pain rather than pain having a handle on me. Pain does not reach the level of magnitude that it once did. I assume that I will have pain in my life, partly because I respect it as a natural experience of life and partly because I am a feeling person. When it arises, I experience it in a manner as healthy and productive as I am able to. Even when I do not feel it immediately, I know that my peace with the pain will eventually come with God's help.

I was never a person who experienced, or maybe allowed myself to experience, much joy in my life. Now I receive joy through a multitude of experiences in life, the greatest of which are through doing God's work and through my awareness of God's numerous blessings in my life. My joy has blossomed from the genuine gratitude I feel in knowing why I am here and what I am to do with this life. Knowing my personal purpose in life and striving to fulfill it bring me authentic joy. My heart sings and soars every time I witness another person grow closer to God. Trey and I are honored to play a part in that process.

I am able to see and feel beauty where I was not able to before. Erin provides a wonderful demonstration of this ability. Instead of clinging to bitterness and anger, she has turned her cancer into an opportunity to share God's love with others. Her celebration of God and willingness to allow God to reach others through her struggle have embraced the hearts of many. One example of her influence can be seen in a group of her friends who were not inclined to share their religious beliefs or spirituality with each other before Erin's cancer diagnosis but have now formed a prayer group on their own accord. They are now supporting and strengthening one another and talking about their spirituality. This is the beauty of God's love.

God has revealed that each of us is love and that He values and loves each of us the same. No matter how good or bad we humans may judge ourselves or others to be, God loves each of us purely and unconditionally, as we are each God's child. The experience of God's love is a blessing that is intended for each of us. Have you ever watched the TV show *Touched by an Angel*? I feel that this show is truly inspired by God. Call us on a Sunday evening at 8 p.m. and you'll hear us sniffling over the message of each and every episode: God loves you.

To understand any emotion wholly, it is beneficial to have a grasp on the opposing emotion. For example, happiness is better understood when it is compared to the experience of sadness. Likewise, our understanding of love is enlightened when we see it within the context of its true polarity. Many of us think that hate is the opposite of love, but in reality, it is fear. Hate stems from fear. *Conversations with God, Book 1*, by Neale Donald Walsch addresses this point much better than I could ever attempt to. *Conversations with God* is incredibly broadening and rich. But we would expect no less from a conversation with God. It fits many of the pieces of life's puzzle neatly and clearly into place. If you haven't already read them, I highly recommend this book and the two sequels when you are open to expanding your spiritual foundation. The following excerpt from Book 1 addresses the relation between love and fear:

> All human actions are motivated at their deepest level by one of two emotions—fear or love. In truth there are only two emotions—only two words in the language of the soul. These are the opposite ends of the great polarity which I [God] created when I produced the universe, and your world, as you know it today.
>
> These are the two points—the Alpha and the Omega—which allow the system you call "relativity" to be. Without these two points, without these two ideas about things, no other idea could exist.
>
> Every human thought, and every human action, is based in either love or fear. There *is* no other human motivation, and

all other ideas are but derivatives of these two. They are simply different versions—different twists on the same theme.

. . .

Fear is the energy which contracts, closes down, draws in, runs, hides, hoards, harms.

Love is the energy which expands, opens up, sends out, stays, reveals, shares, heals.

Fear wraps our bodies in clothing, love allows us to stand naked. Fear clings to and clutches all that we have, love gives all that we have away. Fear holds close, love holds dear. Fear grasps, love lets go. Fear rankles, love soothes. Fear attacks, love amends.

Every human thought, word, or deed is based in one emotion or the other. You have no choice about this, because there is nothing else from which to choose. But you have free choice about which of these to select.

The two people in my life who presently are facing extremely difficult circumstances have each chosen a different path. Although there is more to Carl than fear, he has chosen fear as his response to his troubles. Erin has responded with love.

Amy summarized love well when she said, "That's what we all are—love that must be acknowledged and nurtured and cherished and respected. Love—pure."

Love acknowledged

Love nurtured

Love cherished

Love respected

Love pure

Thank you, Amy. Thank you, God. I know my tears of joy bring you joy.

ELEVEN

Honesty

T REY AND I PROCLAIM TO THE WORLD: WE PLACE GOD = LOVE AND HONESTY FIRST IN OUR LIVES! WE ARE LOVE AND WE ARE HONEST.

So why the need for a public proclamation? Because we feel that this articulation of who and what we are empowers us in two ways: commitment and accountability. By consciously deciding that from this day forward we will live our lives wholly honestly, we have committed to a personal goal, just like setting a financial or career goal. This value and our commitment to it are now tangible and real, which helps us to direct our lives toward this end rather than haphazardly hitting it from time to time. By defining and then committing to who and what we want to be, we ultimately free ourselves to be it and live it. And by taking the extra step of expressly holding ourselves out to our family, friends, and coworkers as honest people, we have not only ourselves as watch guards, but the rest of the world as well. This accountability strengthens our commitment.

Carl comes to mind again in this discussion, as I know him well and have seen his contrasting approach to honesty. Carl is largely consumed with his own interests and is uncaring of the consequences that his actions bring upon others, so the use of dishonesty when it will benefit his personal cause is not an issue for him. Sometimes he'll create or manipulate a gray area to justify his dishonesty, and other times he'll just create his own reality. He even uses other people's dishonesty to justify his own. My husband's response to this latter rationale is that actions that are wrong are no more or less wrong because other people do them. During one conversation, Carl stated that our honest focus was shared by no more than 1 percent of the population. My response to his perception is that like attracts like. He sees the world as dishonest because he is. We see the world as generally honest or at least moving toward that direction because we are and we surround ourselves with like-minded people. Ironically, Carl and other people who choose dishonesty are often intensely angered by people who are dishonest with them. They are also angered by an honest reflection of their own dishonesty. Go figure.

Honesty, in my mind, is black and white. I'm not saying that the consequences of the truth are always black and white, but the truth is the truth, period. Honesty that is manipulated or stretched or used in a piecemeal fashion is not honesty; it is dishonesty.

Honesty is vital in all aspects of our lives, but I'm going to single out personal relationships to explore the subject further. To determine whether two people communicate honestly in their relationship, we tend to focus on the quantity of communication between them. We also tend to think of females as being more communicative than males, although we shouldn't assume that being more talkative means being more truthful. For example, at the outset of Trey's and my relationship, I talked more about our issues, but Trey was more honest in his communications. Although an open line of communication is important in a relationship, it is the quality of the communication, the ability to honestly share feelings, that is vital.

Honesty in a personal relationship can preclude 1) walls from being erected, allowing a relationship to grow if, and where, it is intended to, 2) feelings from being hurt at a deeper level, and 3) guilt from arising. Consequently, honesty saves time and emotional energy and allows us to grow and evolve more quickly because we are less burdened and more emotionally and spiritually healthy.

First, as an example of a barrier being erected, I'd like to share a conversation that occurred over ten years ago after I flunked the bar exam. My mother told me, "Let's just not tell anyone that you failed." Not until after my spiritual experience did I share with her the impact this comment had on me. I knew that my friends would know that I flunked the bar since most of them were lawyers as well. So what I interpreted her statement to mean was that she was embarrassed by me and didn't want *her* friends to know. I felt that she was valuing me by my external accomplishments and failures rather than by the person I was inside. Immediately erected by me: one thick, brick wall in my relationship with my mother.

When I finally shared with her my honest feelings about her response, I learned the true motivation behind her comment. She saw my intense pain and sadness and wanted to help me; she made the comment in her loving desire to ease my pain. I realized that I could have saved myself over a decade of resentment and hurt feelings had I just been honest with her at the time about how I felt. Instead, I created a huge negative that I attached to and wouldn't release, stifling possible growth between my mom and me.

Second, we have all experienced honesty that is painful. Although pain is an emotion we wish to avoid, faced with a painful honest communication or a painless dishonest communication, I will always choose the honest communication and pain. Over time, the pain is less burdensome to our souls than the dishonesty.

An experience with Trey illustrates this point. After two years in a monogamous relationship, I asked Trey where he saw our relationship heading. I was hoping for a definitive response along the lines of if our relationship continued on the path it was on, we would marry. He answered that he saw our marriage as a 50 - 50 probability. This hurt. I had invested my love, focus, and energy in what I felt was a healthy, loving relationship, and I had high hopes and expectations for our future. His view of an equal chance for success or failure anguished me. But eventually, I appreciated knowing his honest feelings. For one thing, his honesty allowed us to discuss why he was at a different place than I was. We were then able to address the aspects of our relationship that needed work. For another thing, I was then fully aware of the risk I was taking going forward. Obviously, our relationship succeeded, but if it had not, I would have been better emotionally prepared for that outcome.

A recent illustration is almost ridiculous, yet these types of scenarios occur all the time. A friend indicated that he was about to fire one of his employees because she was not performing all of the tasks he wanted her to. I asked if he had talked to this woman about his expectations for her. He said he had not because he was uncomfortable criticizing her work. He wanted to avoid conflict and hurting her feelings. I suggested that she would prefer to hear constructive criticism than be let go. Another one of those easy calls when you're not in it! If he let her know what was expected and she failed to do it, then he could let her go. As is clear here, complete honesty also breeds fairness.

In most cases, we instinctively know when we're not being told the truth. Our heart, if not our mind, longs for the truth over dishonesty given to us ostensibly to keep us from getting hurt or because someone thinks that's what we want to hear. Although the communicator may have the best of intentions in hiding the truth, we are far better served by veracity. When, and if, the truth eventually comes to light, we're hurt anyway, usually more deeply than if there had been total honesty from the outset. Just think about all the wasted time and emotional energy spent reading between the lines to get to the truth. In my experience, I found that those times when I had to read between the lines, I rarely discovered the whole truth. I am thankfully at a place in my life where I will directly ask for a person's honest feeling. And I usually know in my heart whether I'm receiving it or not. Honesty allows us to ascertain the real nature of a situation or relationship, so that we can make informed decisions or ask further questions. Honesty protects and empowers us, even when it hurts us.

Third, as the communicator of honest, unfavorable information, we may be pained by hurting another, but we are guilt free and can respect ourselves. Not everything in life is easy, but living up to God's hopes for us by treating all people with love, respect, and honesty gives us great worth and beauty.

Many of us have been in a relationship in which we were not wholly honest with the other person. Ironically for me, I was not wholly honest when I ended my relationship with John, the man who was my personal "savior." I knew in my heart that God did not want us to marry, but I had a difficult time accepting that. It just did not make sense to me, as we truly loved each other and he had brought such beauty to my life. Still I left John but without being honest about the reason. For years, I carried deep-seated guilt over my actions, literally experiencing nightmares over the pain I caused him.

I asked for God's forgiveness too many times to count. And although I knew that God forgave me because I was sorry from the depths of my soul, I still clung to the guilt. God healed me by letting me know that I had to forgive myself to move on. Eventually I did. Reflecting upon this experience, I think I was finally able to forgive myself because I was focused on being an honest person and I knew that I would never mistreat another person as I did John. I am forever sorry that I learned this lesson at his expense. I now know that had I been honest with John at the time, I would still have experienced hurt, but I wouldn't have attached to the guilt. Once again: guilt is a negative, a barrier, that impedes growth.

Before our spiritual experience, I considered Trey and myself to be honest people, as we did not outright lie or purposely deceive, but now I recognize that we were also not eager to confront or address issues. Although we didn't speak falsely, our failure to communicate our whole feelings prevented us from being wholly honest. It is a matter of the degree of honesty. *Conversations with God, Book 2* talks about honesty in terms of visibility. Within that concept is dishonesty by omission. Since our awakening, Trey and I have an impulse to "cut to the chase" and get to the heart of matters; we are, or attempt to be, diplomatically direct with respect to all relationships, personal and professional. *Conversations with God* addresses honesty as follows:

> I [God] tell you this: *nothing* breeds fairness faster than *visibility*.
> *Visibility* is simply another word for *truth*.
> Know the truth and the truth shall set you free.
> . . .
> This is about simply being open and honest in your dealings with another. This is about simply telling the truth when you speak, and about withholding no truth when you know it should be spoken. This is about never again lying, or shading, or verbally or mentally manipulating, or twisting your truth into the hundred and one other contortions which typify the largest number of human communications.
>
> This is about coming clean, telling it like it is, giving it to them straight. This is about ensuring that all individuals have all the data and know everything they need to know on a subject. This is about fairness and openness and, well . . . *visibility*.
>
> Yet this does not mean that every single thought, every private fear, every darkest memory, every fleeting judgment, opinion, or reaction must be placed on the table for discussion

and examination. That is not visibility, that is insanity, and it will make you crazy.

We are talking here about simple, direct, straightforward, open, honest, complete communication. Yet even at that, it is a striking concept, and a little-used one.

During one of our channeling sessions with High Guide, Trey commented that we have felt a freedom to be honest since our spiritual awakening. High Guide responded that there were never any limitations on our honesty. How true, yet we limited ourselves from being wholly honest. Was it our insecurity? Our fear of losing something? Now we have no fear. *There is nothing we can lose by virtue of being honest that we value holding on to.* We are not suggesting that we will cut our ties to every dishonest influence, but we realize that our unmasking of the truth frightens and threatens those who are dishonest, and some may cut their ties with us. We are at peace with that outcome, as we recognize that our time and energy on earth are too precious to uphold and corroborate dishonesty, whether through a personal relationship or a professional one. We have to keep in mind not to attack with honesty, nor to disguise our fear as honesty. If we communicate honestly *from love*, then we will not attack or intentionally hurt another.

My husband uses the following hypothetical as a method of focusing on honesty in the work environment:

> If you had a choice, which work environment would you choose? A company where you have to work within a political paradigm of getting ahead by making yourself and your boss look good, maybe by controlling information and competing against coworkers—where you are forced to protect your own turf, in effect? Or a company where the focus is on the common, collective good, where open communication and collective effort are recognized and rewarded, where

valuable contributions can come from any person, regardless of that person's role?

Most people say they would choose the latter, but the former is more prevalent. Why?

Trey's response to his hypothetical is that although we want the open, honest workplace, we choose the political model because we are afraid to be the fool. So, collectively, we *create* these political environments through our volitional choices, though we rarely see it that way. Rather than blaming the dynamic of our work environments on some external, nonexistent influence, we need to recognize, and take responsibility for, everything we create through our own choices.

My feeling is that our society as a whole is shortsighted. We think that there is not enough to go around of whatever it is that we're searching for. So we tend to be selfish and greedy and look out for our own self-interests at the expense of others. But I can't help but think how limited, and how limiting, that attitude is. You have a child and you love that child with all your heart. When your second child is born, do you have any love remaining for the new child? Of course you do. Our love is unlimited. And the gifts of life, both physical and internal, are more than abundant to provide for every soul on earth. Everyone involved benefits when the focus is on the collective good.

I have to admit that frustration arises when I think about how so many of our businesses and governments operate. For some reason, we feel it is okay to lower our moral standards in the professional or public arena. Maybe it is the power and security of group mentality, or maybe it is the anonymity and lack of personal accountability. Whatever the reason, we place our priority on getting a bigger piece of the pie, and in doing so, we tend to ignore the needs of others, not to accept when we have enough, and to see ourselves in competition against others.

Competition can have one of two very different faces: that of the destruction of our competitors, or that of motivation and growth.

Sometimes it seems that collectively we are choosing to align ourselves against one another rather than with one another, that we have come to believe that for one of us to win, another must lose. We then manipulate the playing field with dishonesty and dirty tactics, trying to gain any possible advantage and enhance our own self-interests. That approach is not working to make the world a better place for all people. We can, however, reap productive and positive results even in competition by shifting our focus from self-interests to collective good. With this shift, honest competition can motivate us to focus on and learn better ways to produce, to serve, and to live.

Honesty needs to cross all borders. I admit that it seems an almost insurmountable challenge for each of us individually to effect change in this world, but our courage to be honest immediately benefits our own lives and the lives of those who witness it. Although largely unseen, an even broader impact occurs when we shift from dishonesty to honesty, in that our collective consciousness is raised to a higher level. We can truly make a difference in our lives and the lives of others by choosing a loving, respectful, honest path, and the world will be a far better place thereby, one person, one step, at a time.

TWELVE

Clearing and Cleansing

I LOVE THE CONCEPT BEHIND THE PROCESSES I am about to describe. They came to me soon after my experience. I was reflecting on my life to determine how I had gotten to such a wonderful place: a place where I was emotionally and spiritually healthy and where Jesus would act so directly in my life and have me write a book for Him. I haven't always been this open and healthy, so how did I get here? I got here through the processes of clearing and cleansing.

CLEARING: We remove the veils, layers, and falsities that mask our authentic self. These veils are created by ourselves, although we are influenced by our family, our friends, and society. Upon removing these veils, we are at a place of *self-awareness*. We see the reality of who we are, both positive and negative. We are identifying our true self.

CLEANSING: Once we have identified some or all of our true self, we are able to work on eliminating our negative aspects and on bringing more good and positives into our life. When we cleanse ourselves of our negatives, we eliminate our self-created and self-permitted barriers to growth, freeing ourselves to evolve along a path of higher energies, and we direct our life toward love and its many positive derivatives. We are engaged in the process of *self-growth*, bettering ourselves with our intent and focus on love and goodness.

Clearing and cleansing are lifelong processes that will typically overlap. You don't have to clear all of your issues before you can cleanse any particular one of them. You may find yourself simultaneously in both processes depending upon the issues you're working on. And you may be able to see the reality of some issues without needing to clear them, allowing you to begin with the cleansing process. So it is beneficial to understand that there is no one correct path to these processes, and that every person's method of applying them is as individualized as the life and experiences of that person.

Although I feel that I generally went through a reflective, clearing mode in my teens and twenties and that I am now in a cleansing mode, I have issues that pop up from time to time that I must work on clearing. Sometimes my veil is newly-created, sometimes it has been buried so deep that I am unable to see it until I peel away another veil on top of it, and other times I simply do not have an awareness of the issue until a life experience brings it to my attention. I have been amazed at the depth of the layers that I have created from my fear, from assuming the standards dictated by others, and from the painful experiences in my life. It is a common occurrence for me to peel away a veil and find another one underneath, needing to be stripped.

Self-awareness is merely complete honesty with yourself. Imagine removing yourself, or your ego, from yourself and objectively examining who that person is, who you are, without emotional attachment to the positives or shortcomings of that person. As an outsider looking in, you could objectively identify the reality of your personality or self. Now imagine reuniting with yourself while maintaining your honesty, your objectivity. You could simply be aware of your positives without enhancing your ego and be aware of your negatives without diminishing your self-worth and without using those negative attributes as excuses. You now understand that you are who you are, not who you thought you were or who you wished you were or who others thought you to be. Never again will you choose to hide from yourself or camouflage your true self. In this way, you relinquish your internal judge, the voice that feeds and eats away at your sense of self. You release your ego.

Self-awareness is the window to your true self in relation to both the physical world and God's world. Those characteristics that honor your beauty, you can celebrate as gifts from God. God is honored by your humility. Those traits that disappoint or displease you or that fail to measure up to who you desire to be, you can strive to change.

When we engage in the processes of clearing and cleansing, of self-awareness and self-growth, we enhance our connection with God, whether we're focused on that connection or not. Increased self-awareness chips away at the walls that block our relationships, spawning growth in those relationships, including our relationship with the Divine. This holds true even for those who do not recognize their personal relationship with God, as clearing and cleansing direct us down a path of betterment and goodness, which is the path of God.

For example, even though Trey did not feel any personal relationship with God when we married, he was very focused on bringing more good into his life. He had already learned that when you start making good decisions, the ripple effect carries you deeper into goodness. Life becomes simpler and more beautiful. Obstacles no longer send you over the edge because everything else in your life is "together," making you both stronger and better equipped to deal with crisis. Life is not perceived as burdensome or a test, but rather as the experience that you make of it. Even though Trey was not consciously or purposely focused on the Creator, he eventually grew close to Him. His focus on self-betterment through goodness opened his heart and enabled him to see God within himself and others.

Clearing brings us the awareness that allows us to see the honesty and truth in ourselves, in others, and in situations so that we can cleanse and grow. And with awareness comes simplification. Appropriate actions and resolutions to problems become clearer. That is not to say that following through with those actions and resolutions is always easy, but at least the course of action is more obvious.

In my case, each process generally coincided with one of the two intimate relationships in my life. Although I had begun questioning who I was before John entered my life, I associate him with the process of clearing because of our youthful age and the length of our relationship. We started dating when we were seventeen. He was my sole (and soul) companion for five years and then off and on for an additional three years. John was an integral part of my life during my "Who am I?" years, the period when I first turned within to examine the internal me, the real me. He helped me to remove the "sins" of my biological father from myself: I was not bad because my father's actions were bad; I was who I was based solely on my intent and my actions. John saw much good in me and helped bring that to my awareness. With this awareness, I began to gain a sense of worthiness, worthiness to be loved by another as well as worthiness to give my love to him and others. When I finally recognized the veils that disguised my goodness, those of shame, guilt, and unworthiness that I had created because of my father's negative influence in my life, I was able to begin the long process of removing them.

Looking back at our relationship, I am amazed that John stayed with me for so long, as he was occasionally the target of my attacks. It was as if I were daring him to leave me, partly because I had felt abandoned in the past by those who loved me, and partly because it took many years for me to accept my worthiness. Because of my feelings of unworthiness, I tended to reject the love, goodness, and beauty in my life; I subconsciously felt that I didn't deserve those gifts. I will always

Clearing and Cleansing

be grateful to John for his understanding, patience, and love, all of which supported and strengthened me in the journey to heal my soul.

Through my self-examination over time, I was able to remove other veils masking my true self. I saw that I wasn't what clothes I wore, what I looked like, what my grades were, or who my family and friends were, but who I was inside, the good and the bad. I was on the right path, although there was still much work to be done.

There are a myriad of ways to awaken your self-awareness so that you are able to see the veils you have created. Take note of and examine your feelings and actions that you are uncomfortable with and tend to set aside. Consider recurring criticism from friends, family members, co-workers, and significant others. Investigate why you blame others for your unhappiness or predicament or why you feel threatened by the talents, money, or success of another individual. Seek counseling to uncover dysfunctional patterns in your behavior. Use meditation as a path for turning inside. Pray to God to illuminate your negatives. Journal your deepest fears and pain. Journaling can be extremely productive because it is an active process of releasing and purging and it is private, which does not put you on the defensive or threaten you. If you are honest in your journaling, you will begin to see the real you. Trusting your intuition is imperative with all of these approaches. For example, when you are criticized, your intuition can help you to discern whether it is your issue or an issue of the person criticizing you.

Uncovering your fears and the negative aspects of yourself can make you feel weak and vulnerable. Rather than seeing yourself as weak, recognize that you are actually strong for having the courage to confront those fears. You empower yourself through self-awareness.

My cleansing process took off with Trey's presence in my life. I had never met a person with a higher level of integrity or fairness than Trey. And he not only preached the talk, but also lived the talk. I became a better person by virtue of witnessing his goodness, as he was an example of how to bring more goodness into my life as well as an example of how beautiful life can be.

I personally found it beneficial to discover the origin of the negative aspects of myself, that is, the WHY and HOW I attached to the negative. Understanding the why and how helped me in two ways: 1) I could eliminate some of the guilt or burden of the negative, and 2) I could see what to do to eliminate the negative or prevent it from recurring. As Freud recognized so clearly, almost every negative we attach to arises from experiences in our past, particularly in our childhood.

Growth through cleansing can be hindered and complicated by a lack of awareness of why you have the negatives that you have. It is beneficial to have a starting point of reference in order to have a finish-line goal. How can you eliminate the bad if you don't know why you possess it? For example, assume that you are having trouble in relationships. One path to solve this problem is just to eliminate bad relationships in your life. Another path is to decide that you are going to make your relationships better; you won't be jealous anymore or angry anymore, or maybe you won't take verbal abuse from your mate anymore. These two approaches are merely band-aid approaches, treating the symptoms rather than the cause. Ending a relationship because of verbal abuse, for example, only temporarily solves the problem. Odds are that you will enter into another relationship of abuse. And deciding to just end your own detrimental behavior can be a long and difficult endeavor because of the ingrained and habitual nature of the negative.

The more effective path would be to see where all your weaknesses or downfalls are in relationships and then instead of just deciding to change them, identify why you are that way. Examine why you take abuse or abuse others—because you feel unworthy or insecure. And why are you unworthy or insecure? Perhaps your dad made you feel that no matter what you did, it wasn't good enough, or your mom never told you she loved you, or when your dad divorced your mom, he divorced you too, or you were really overweight as a child and continuously ridiculed, or your brother died and your parents shut you out, or you grew up poor around much hostility and fear, or you grew up wealthy with hired nannies raising you, or your sibling was better than you at everything, or you just didn't get the attention you needed because there were five kids in your family, or your dad was always working and never did anything with you . . . . Behind every personal negative is a personal truth. With knowledge of that truth, you can begin to rebuild yourself.

It is important to distinguish between finding the reason and finding an excuse. It is not acceptable to fall back on "Well, this happened to me in my life, and that's just the way I am—take it or leave it." Such a response is an excuse that impedes cleansing. As an example, imagine you are in a relationship where your mate expresses concern about your irrational jealousy and fear of commitment. You realize that you are that way because the person in your prior relationship cheated on you. If you tell your mate that he or she must accept you that way, you are making an excuse. If you see the prior dishonesty as the cause of your jealousy and fear, understand the negative impact of your behavior, and want to change, then you are finding the reason, which can help you to grow. Although you were a victim, you can choose not to lead the rest of your life as one. You can learn from the experience, grow from it, and choose not to inflict your victimization on others and, most important, yourself.

I think most of us know in our hearts what behavior is helpful and what is hurtful. We know that we should treat others with honesty and respect. Yet we often fail to hold ourselves to the "right" or "higher" standards. Our failures are grounded in a variety of reasons or excuses such as selfishness, jealousy, insecurity, anger, "I'll never see them again," "that's who I am," "burn the bridge because I was wronged," and so on. We tend to take our higher path when it is easy but not when it is difficult. And it is easy to overlook our higher path when we have been slighted or wronged, because we feel we have the right to lash back. Hurting others, even when we feel that we are justified in principle, hurts our soul. If we direct our lives to act and react with love, then no matter the simplicity or complexity of the issue, or the ease or difficulty of dealing with the issue, or the depth of pain caused us by the issue, we will grow and evolve by walking down the path that God has intended for us to take. If we wish to grow and evolve, we must commit to striving for the right or higher path and not allow excuses or laziness to deter us.

Cleansing is a matter of taking responsibility for who we are. There is comfort in the excuse because it is easier to blame others than to change ourselves. Changing who we are can be scary. We must confront our weaknesses and own up to our part in creating them. Sometimes we are even unsure whether we can successfully better ourselves. And change and growth are usually not instantaneous but require continued effort and focus on our part. All of these fears can impede our self-betterment—but only when we give them that power. Ultimately, we are faced with deciding whether to heal, grow, and improve or to continue imposing our negativity, dysfunction, and pain on ourselves and others.

Figuring out the origin of your negative is only part of the cleansing process. The final step lies in eliminating the negative. You can use techniques outlined by professionals, or you can create your own method. No matter the approach, praying for God's assistance and guidance will always help. I was fortunate that I was able to clear and cleanse many of my issues without professional help. Counselors weren't as accessible in schools when I was growing up, nor was there the volume of self-help books that exists today. I recommend seeking professional help if you feel that the task is greater than you can accomplish alone. I know I would have been a healthier person much sooner had I sought counseling.

It is also helpful to bring to your awareness, that is to consciously conceptualize and articulate, exactly who it is you want to be and where you want to go. When you couple awareness of the standard you are striving for with awareness of why you are failing to reach that standard, you set in motion a more directed focus for cleansing.

A few years back, I went to the funeral of a mother of a close friend. I didn't know my friend's mother well when she was alive, but after her funeral I sure did. She was a teacher, and her positive influence on so many students' lives was abundantly evident. I left that funeral hoping that when my life is over, I will have left some lives enriched. This woman's life, although not directly involved in mine, made a mark on mine by prompting me to decide who I wanted to be.

I'm going to share with you a clearing and cleansing of one aspect of myself of which I am not proud. Earlier I mentioned my attacks on John—daring him to leave me, in effect. Well, I continued those attacks on Trey. Trey eventually told me that he could not marry me if I did not get rid of my anger. It is amazing to me now, but I did not see myself as being angry or having a temper. I didn't throw objects, or hit him or other things, or put my hand through a wall or window, or get thrown out of restaurants, or shoot up my kitchen, or throw clothes into the fire, or threaten to kill anyone . . . as my biological father had done, so I didn't see myself as out of control. What I did do every time we had a fight that struck a chord of pain within me (that is, approached my insecurity or fear of abandonment) was lash back with angry, hurtful words. He hurt me, so I had to hurt him back.

I became aware through clearing that I possessed a deep-rooted anger. I had veiled my anger so well that it was invisible to me. Trey's honesty triggered my honest reflection of my feelings and actions, enabling me to see—for the first time—the anger that I had possessed for years. Anger expressed through words can hurt and scar as severely as physical anger. I learned that lesson in my childhood, yet I continued that cycle in my adult life. Trey and I explored all the facets of my anger so that I could see the true reality of it. I came to see my anger as a self-defense mechanism that originated from the pain of my childhood.

Once we both understood why I had anger, we worked on eliminating it. For the first time, I consciously focused on what I felt when I was angry. By going to my anger, I became aware of how it played on my emotions. In other words, I had to go and shake hands with my anger and get to know it better before I could send it on its way. I shared the dynamic of my anger with Trey.

When I was angry, I lost all common sense, perspective, and mental control. I felt this wave come over me that was similar to going into shock, like I was in a dream. Crazy thoughts went through my head, all focused on hurting the "hurter." Most of the time I wasn't even aware of everything I said. And it was worse if I had been drinking. The ironic part is that what I longed for more than anything when I was pushing the hurter—Trey or John—away was for him to hold me and tell me he loved me and that everything was going to be okay. As you can imagine, a loving response is almost impossible from any person who is being attacked. I thought that if he really loved me, he wouldn't leave the room or drive away no matter what I said. And when he did leave, I felt abandoned all over again. Although it seemed illogical to verbally lash out at him, yet internally cry out for his love, affection, and security, at least now we knew the reality of my anger as a response to being hurt.

So Trey and I literally made a deal. When I began to feel the wave of anger and loss of control coming over me, I would let Trey know that I was starting to lose it. No matter where we were in our argument, how mad we were, how strongly I felt I was in the right, I would tell him, and he would reach out his hand to me. I would then take his hand, and we would stop talking. It had to be difficult for Trey to always be the one to extend his hand and make the peace offering. I now see how Trey's hand of peace embodied the unselfish essence of love. Inevitably, a few moments later, we would hug, and I would cry. This may sound silly, but it worked. Together we disarmed my anger. I received the security and comfort of his love at the moment I needed it most. And I didn't have to fear his leaving me or not loving me.

Over time, I shed my fear of abandonment, and with that shedding, I released my anger. Now Trey and I have no problem arguing any issue to the end, unless I throw in a curse word because of my

Clearing and Cleansing

frustration arguing with an articulate attorney! Then I'm just immature, of course.

It is unlikely that any of us will see our pure, 100 percent true selves or ever reach the point of perfection. But over the course of our lives, we can come close to our true selves through clearing, and we can get to a point of "fine-tuning" ourselves through cleansing. When you are able to see that there are no longer big, significant issues, but merely small, almost innocuous concerns that you are working on, then you have reached the fine-tuning place. And that is a wonderful place to be.

Every one of us has baggage, but what we hold on to is solely within our control. We alone must choose whether to burden our life by carrying the baggage with us, or whether to lighten our load by putting it down.

THIRTEEN

Creating False Realities

WE CANNOT EXPECT TO ACCOMPLISH any significant clearing unless we can begin to see the realities of our relationships more honestly. From a spiritual perspective, relationships are just mirrors that show us the different aspects of ourselves. If we never understand that, and all of its implications, then we are more likely to continue creating and maintaining the veils that camouflage our true selves.

A couple of common ways we create false realities are through projection and assumption. Projection is simply ascribing to others one's own ideas, impulses, or emotions, without being aware of doing so. Understanding projection helps us to identify whether a negative trait we perceive in a person is actually a reflection of our own negative trait. As an example, you may perceive a friend to be materialistic because she has a more expensive home and car, and she takes lavish vacations. When you investigate why you have that perception, you realize that you are envious of her possessions and that you really want the things she has. You discover that you yourself are the one who is materialistic. The idea behind uncovering your acts of projection is not to determine whether another person has a certain trait, but to take a closer look at yourself.

Through assumption we take on—or assume—the negative trait of another. During my adolescence, I took on the guilt for my biological father's negative acts. I saw myself as bad because my father was bad. In reality, his behavior should not have had any bearing on my identity or self-worth, but I assumed his negatives anyway.

Other examples of ways that we create false realities are more subtle, but just as prevalent. Here are a couple of examples where, upon taking an honest look at my interactions with others, I saw myself, the real me, more clearly.

The first relationship involved a priest at our former church. He is very scholarly and well read, and his communications are always articulate and insightful. When I was around him, I felt intimidated. For a couple of years, I perceived him to be unapproachable and a little pretentious. Eventually I noticed that Trey and other parishioners were not intimidated by him. That awareness prompted me to look deeper into my negative perception of him. I recognized that I felt threatened by his positive traits because they highlighted my own perceived weaknesses. I did not see myself as well read, and I was unsure of my ability to clearly communicate my thinking, especially in a public speaking situation. I was able to see that, in reality, the priest was not unapproachable, pretentious, or intimidating at all. I falsely created the impression of those negative qualities in him rather than accept and acknowledge my own insecurities. I veiled my negatives because it was easier for me to label another person with negative traits than to own up to my own.

Another way I have created a false reality occurred in my relationship with Trey. On the morning of my Jesus encounter when Trey and I were still in bed, I shared with Trey insights about our underlying relationship that neither of us had ever brought to the surface before. With this new insight, I became aware of my self-defeating reaction to one of Trey's negatives. Trey had allowed his strength and independence to deter him from opening totally to me. Without seeing how my own fear played a role in the process, I had subconsciously closed off a piece of myself to him. I had also wrongly placed all the blame on Trey for the last vestige of distance in our relationship. His negative in its own right should not have prevented me from loving him wholly or committing to him completely. Had I been more in tune with my feelings of unworthiness and my fear of rejection and abandonment, I could have responded to Trey more healthily and honestly by helping him to remove his wall rather than pushing him away with a wall of my own.

We often create false realities on a subconscious level, as we are acting without awareness of our negative traits or of how we allow another person's traits to trigger our negative traits. We are more likely to distort and misperceive our interactions and relationships with others when we are blind to our true selves. Opening our eyes to reality is not always easy. Understanding that we can and do hide from ourselves is a starting place. When a negative emotion arises, we can take the opportunity to look for the truth. We must connect with ourselves and see the reality of who we are, both the healthful and harmful aspects, in order to live honestly and consciously.

Even when we are living honestly and with awareness, we sometimes create false negatives or veils within ourselves because of abuse or victimization. A few years ago, I saw an interview of Maya Angelou that helps illustrate this point. Angelou addressed the question of how women who have been raped could emotionally and psychologically handle that victimization and keep from assuming responsibility for it, believing that they somehow caused or invited the rape. Her instruction that stuck with me was for the victim to understand and feel "I'm not in it." A rape occurs solely because of the negatives and issues of the rapist. It has nothing to do with the victim's personality, traits, or characteristics, as a rapist will rape one woman as easily as another. So one way that a rape victim can begin to deal with the crime is to separate who she is from the rape itself: "I'm not in it—it's not about me."

Awareness that no correlation exists between herself and the act of rape or the negatives of the rapist can empower the victim. By seeing where we have responsibility—and where we don't—we can avoid the often devastating consequences of the unhealthy dynamics we otherwise might set in motion. We can all learn from Angelou's advice. Overwhelming pain inflicted on us can confuse and blur reality, resulting in our taking responsibility when we should not. Understanding when we're "not in it" can help us see through that confusion so that we don't create a negative of our own.

We create false realities by acting out of fear rather than love. The truth can be difficult to recognize through our convolution and manipulation. When we choose to look at ourselves and our interactions with others through honest and aware eyes, we can begin to peel away the false layers that we have created and we can avoid adding new layers. Whenever an encounter with an individual arouses a negative emotion in me now, instead of labeling or judging that person as negative, I look inside myself to see what and where my issues are that cause me to feel threatened by that person. I now recognize that each and every one of my negative emotions originates solely within me. And I must find the root of each one if I wish to weed it out.

FOURTEEN

Free Will and the Game of Life

WHY DOESN'T GOD GIVE US CONCRETE SIGNS of His existence and Heaven? Why does He allow bad things, even horrific things, to happen? The underlying reason, as many of us have heard before, is that God gives us free choice, free will. Through free will, God allows us ultimate freedom. We all choose how to live our lives and who it is we want to be, without God either preventing us from having what we choose or changing what we choose. This is a beautiful gift. Yet it is also a gift that complicates our human experience and understanding of God.

I have long felt that there is an attribute of gamesmanship to our earthly experience. We're born on earth with all memory of our preexistence with God erased. We trudge along, hopefully rediscovering God and that we are love, and that our purpose is to evolve to pure love. A roll of the dice? It can seem that way.

I feel that I have a glimpse of understanding of some aspects of this "game of rediscovery." For instance, I believe that God shows us the highest honor through His gift of free will. And I believe that we value more intensely that which we discover and learn on our own.

Free Will and the Game of Life

Still there remain aspects of this game that I do not fully grasp. At times it seems as if the rules are stacked against us. We're put on this physical, material plane and then expected to see through, and past, the tangible and solid in order to experience ourselves and God through the intangibles of intuition and faith. Here is where I acknowledge that I am a child unable to understand all of God's grand scheme. Here is where I trust that the rules of His game are for our best interest and higher purpose. Yet even with that trust, I try to analyze and fit it all together.

Knowing that we are unable to comprehend and see the whole of God, Her universe and Her workings, I can speak only in generalizations, appreciating that there are exceptions to those generalizations. I categorize God's interactions in our lives in two ways: internal and external. Continuing with the "game of rediscovery" analogy, we can look at life as a team sport with humans as the players and God as the coach. The coach doesn't come into the game and play it for us but is always on the sidelines with helpful advice. Sometimes we choose to listen to the coach and other times we don't, but the coach is always there. To put it another way, God (generally) does not act externally in our lives, but is always available for us internally.

God doesn't intend for bad things to happen. I don't believe that when a child dies, for instance, it is necessarily God's will or purpose. Neither does God step in and make things "right" for us. She doesn't prevent emotional or physical abuse, war, murders, natural disasters that take many lives, disease, the Holocaust, drug abuse . . . . She doesn't send money or fame our way. Coach allows us to use everything we have to deal with all of the factors and elements surrounding us. But She allows the game to play out as it will.

Even so, I believe that, at times, God does suit up and step in to change the course of free will in action. We have all heard stories of miracles attributed to God and Her angels. And I believe that we agree to some struggles before our incarnation on earth to serve God's purpose in our own life or the lives of others. Erin believes that she agreed to her cancer before her earthly birth so that she would have the opportunity to share her relationship with God with many others. (But then again, maybe she randomly got cancer and then discovered a great purpose for it.)

A favorite phrase of a female minister at our old church was that GOD ACTS IN HISTORY FOR A PURPOSE. Only after my spiritual experience did I come to understand this statement. She was referring to God's external interaction in our lives. When I read the Christmas story to my children, I feel the beauty and astonishment that the shepherds must have felt upon their encounter with the angels, because I too have had direct contact with God and His world. God outwardly acted in my life so that I could be a messenger of His love. He showed me that I am love and He helped me to accept the love in my life, enabling me to help others to do the same. And He outwardly acts in other people's lives for other purposes, which are always His purposes. These external interactions appear to occur infrequently and to be largely beyond our control. I do believe, however, that we have the power to prompt God to change the course of history through mass, collective prayer. When you think about it, mass, collective prayer is simply collective free will in action.

We have no guarantee that we will live our lives free from danger or tragedy. In fact, we know otherwise. But we do have the guarantee that no matter what we are faced with in life, God will help us deal with it if we ask Him. When we turn to God in prayer and focus, we become able to see God acting every day, every moment, in our lives. He will heal and strengthen our souls every time. He will help us to better ourselves. He will show us His answers to our prayers. Of course, God's answers to our prayers are not always what we wish. We may feel abandoned or ignored. When we feel neglected, we should recognize that God's answers gratify our souls' needs, not necessarily our earthly needs and desires. Only when we truly understand that God is love, and that His answers always serve love, will we wholly see and accept God's internal assistance. Trust God and His answers. Trust your feelings, your heart, where God truly does talk to you. God speaks; just listen.

So we should proceed in this game of rediscovery guided by the "rules" we do know. Generally, God does not overrule, or change the course of, free will. She allows us each and every choice that we make, yet we should be mindful that our choices are not insignificant, as there are karmic consequences with every decision. Although by appearances God rarely intervenes outwardly in the physical world, miracles can and do occur, and *God acts in history for a purpose.* Some of the negative events in our lives occur accidentally or randomly, some by the free will of ourselves or others, and some are agreed to before our birth to serve God's (and thus our own) higher purpose. We may find ourselves searching for the true cause of our struggle. Those times that I am unable to find the cause of an event or situation, I remind myself that I have agreed to all of life's experiences by virtue of choosing the earthly, human experience. I also recognize that my response is at least as important as the cause.

Internally, God is always with us and there for us, helping us to better direct our own lives—if we ask and listen. She wants to be our coach in life, but we must use our free will to allow Her to guide us. Like a great coach, God can give us tools to accomplish things that are far beyond our expectations or our abilities without Her assistance. And we know that God doesn't act or answer according to our earthly desires, but rather through love in harmony with our highest purpose. So we should listen with an open heart and release our expectations and agendas. Finally, through our own choices, we have enormous creative power, God-given power, that is inherent and always available to us. We have more control over our lives than we often realize.

God gave us free will as a means to define who we are, to discover our immense, creative power when we tap into love, and to awaken to our divine nature. Our freedom of choice, of discovery, is one of God's greatest gifts. When we freely give our will back to God, that is, when we choose God's highest purpose for ourselves, we begin to unleash some of our tremendous potential—for the benefit of us all.

FIFTEEN

Spirituality and Religion

Clearing The Veils Of Organized Religion

I have attended church for most of life. For many years, I viewed churches as the only houses of God, organized religion as the only path to God, and Catholic priests as holier, almost less human, than laymen. I didn't consciously decide that those were my views, I just didn't consider otherwise. To me, religion and God were one and the same, so it never occurred to me to challenge my assumptions or to explore the possibility of another reality. For the most part, religion and God were a Sunday morning routine, which like other routines established by my parents early in life, I had accepted and continued without question.

Although my personal exploration of the relation between religion and God has been a gradual process, my quest has enabled me to more clearly recognize them as separate. I strive to understand organized religion in all its beauty and imperfections so that I can gain the benefits that it has to offer and avoid the pitfalls. I feel that many of us are uncomfortable identifying and acknowledging the limitations of religion, and yet it is through our awareness of them that we can clear the veils, the misconceptions, that distance us from our experience of God.

Organized religion is similar to any organization that includes a great number of people in that the organization itself often takes on a life of its own, just as we see with governments and large corporations. The agenda and beliefs of any particular religion can become institutionalized, and possibly bureaucratic and impersonal, which can lend them the appearance of significant credibility and power. Sometimes we are susceptible to the pervasive authoritative influence of religion, causing us to distrust or deny our personal connection with God. We might accept outright what we are told because religion told us so, or believe that we need religion or a religious official as an intermediary for us to come together with God and to learn His truth. In my view, these are damaging misconceptions, for God resides within each of us and His truth is revealed through self-discovery in our relationship with Him. If there were no religions in the world, no Bible or other holy texts, we would not be God-less, because God exists, and we could still grow with Him, because our growth occurs through our personal, internal experience of God.

I have always been troubled by religious teachings of exclusivity. Is X religion the only true religion? Are X people God's only chosen people? I believe not. We are all God's people. We articulate this truth in numerous ways: we possess a kernel of God, we possess the seed of God, we are part God, we are created in the image of God, we possess a spark of God, we are love . . . . The exclusive beliefs of "chosen" churches and "chosen" people stem from fear. These churches and people seem to be seeking the guarantee and support of others to believe they will make the cut to get into Heaven.

In our society, many of us pass judgment on others on the basis of whether they are Christian or not. But we don't stop there. We can break down Christianity into its numerous denominations and witness judgments between factions of our own faith. The same thing happens within Judaism and Islam. It is absurd to me how we "religious people" cling to judgment and prejudice with respect to other religions and denominations.

I find it helpful to look at organized religions as schools where the experiences, knowledge, interpretations, and beliefs of human beings, both past and present, are accumulated and presented to us for insightful consideration. Individuals can sift through the accumulated information and accept the principles that ring true for them. From my experience in life, I have come to the view that few people (including the clergy) actually believe and accept all of the dogma in their chosen religion. Instead, we tend to settle with the religion that most closely aligns with our beliefs or that has been chosen for us. Yet I also recognize that religion does a great service in bringing like-minded people together where God's work can be accomplished individually and collectively.

I believe that the Bible was inspired by God and that God's truth can be learned from it. But I also believe that we should not extrapolate from there to assume or believe that other religions do not see the truth. There are numerous religions in the world, the major ones being followed by millions of people. There is also more than one holy text in this world that is believed to be the "word" of God and the "way" to God. God wants every soul to seek and know the truth. Is it not conceivable that He has inspired the truth in many different people, in many different religions, over the course of time and history?

A multitude of religions exist because Mankind has been unable to form a consensus in its conceptualization of God. God is so vast that we cannot know God as we are able to know other things. Although we are unable to wholly define God, we are able to experience God. Because God is so encompassing, we each experience Him in our own unique way, which is beautiful.

We hunger for the truth, and in our desire to learn the truth, we record the events in the lives of our masters, those people who have mastered God's truth in their lives. We study the masters' lives and experiences, their teachings and insights, and we emulate them and strive for our own mastery. I long for the day when instead of feeling threatened by other religions, we see the benefit of bringing the insights of all major religions together so that we are truly offered the most inclusive and extensive experience of God.

My hope is that we can use religion for its opportunity to broaden our spirits, not as an influence that starts us down that path but then leads us to disempower ourselves. Religion is merely a tool to help us seek God. It is not the end to be seeking—God is. So I suggest that we do not seek religion, but rather seek God through religion.

Having stated that, I'm going to entertain an idea that seemingly contradicts my instruction to seek God. Many of us tend to think that if we follow the right path, whether it be religion or something else, we will find what we are seeking, we will find God. The reality is that we don't need to seek, as we are already there, we just don't realize it. Dorothy in *The Wizard of Oz* sought a means to get home, only to discover that she possessed the ability all along. God is here, not just there. God is now, not just then. God is inside, not just outside. Rather than putting your efforts into seeking God, relax and experience Her within yourself, within nature, within others, as She is around you always and everywhere.

Sin And Forgiveness: Going . . . Going . . . Gone

In my experience in the Catholic church, an inordinate amount of the focus in the services was directed towards sin. I remember leaving the services often feeling burdened with guilt and unworthiness, rather than energized by a joyous celebration of God. The church's fixation with sin and its harsh judgment that I allowed to be rendered upon me caused me to unhealthily attach to my sins. My growth with God was gravely limited by this attachment because I could not see myself as good enough, or righteous enough, to commune with God. I was a sinner, and although I believed God forgave me for my sins, I felt that my sins distanced me from God. It was as if my sinning created a deep gorge between me and God and the only way I could build a bridge connecting me to God was by sinning no more. This absurdity in my mind illustrated the twisted manipulative power of my guilt and unworthiness.

I'm not sure when, but slowly I began to shed the church's judgment and to trust my own. I knew my heart and, more important, God did too. I discovered a compassionate God, unconditionally forgiving of my sins and boundlessly patient with my imperfections. And then Jesus helped me to release any remnants of my attachment to sin with His words: "Guilt is a barrier to growth, but awareness is an impetus for growth. You [we] must strive for perfection, yet be accepting of your [our] faults."

I also remember my dad refusing to take communion because he had not confessed his sins to a priest since his last communion. Even then, I could not fathom any situation when the church should require confession to a priest. Now I recognize that if we enter into ritualistic confession, fully understanding the dynamic of the undertaking and our own essence, our confession to another who is focused on love can be incredibly healing and clarifying. But I struggled with the other implications of ritualized confession.

When I participated in confession, I did so because it was required by the church before something else could take place. I did not participate out of need or desire. My heart was not in it, so my participation was valueless. Further, performing the penitences the priest suggested, such as a certain number of Hail Marys, did not absolve my sin, as there was no correlation between the priest's suggestions and my actions.

We alone know what is in our heart and the course of action that we need to follow to heal ourselves. A priest is an educated counsel who can provide guidance in our search for healing. We should consider his suggestions, but since we each have our own experiences, we should also trust our own insight and intuition.

The more I focused on the ritual of confession, the more I felt that the church seemed to be telling me that my own confession to God was not good enough and that the only way to be truly forgiven was to confess through the priest and the church. By allowing the imposition of an intermediary between us and God, we can permit ourselves to be disempowered, especially if we believe that we cannot directly connect with God and that we are separate from God. This false sense of separation camouflages our essence as a wonderful part of God.

So how do we receive God's healing grace of forgiveness? I used to view forgiveness only through the religious lens—forgiveness was the natural result of confession and repentance. In fact, my healing encounter with Jesus occurred in a religious context, as that was my frame of reference at the time. Within this perspective of sin and forgiveness, confession and repentance are our responsibility in the process and forgiveness comes from both God and ourselves.

Specifically, through genuine confession and remorse, we fully acknowledge the wrong, we make a sincere effort to correct the wrong if that is possible, and we endeavor not to repeat the wrong in order to better ourselves. Religion teaches us that our heartfelt confession and repentance always result in forgiveness from God.

Although this was my model of forgiveness for many years—and much of it still rings true—I now view sin and forgiveness as somewhat paradoxical. While I still believe that it is through taking responsibility for our actions that we properly address the harm that we have done to ourselves or others, I now see that sin and forgiveness effectively have no relevance in God's eyes, as God is allowing us to do what we want to do and be who we want to be. The actions that society or religion judges as wrong or sinful are instead just choices we make to be less than who we are meant to be. As I stated in a previous chapter, sin is a choice against love and our soul's highest interests that negatively affects our soul's evolution. I feel that God does not judge us as sinners for these negative choices, but gives us the freedom to make them, because it is through these choices and their consequences that we eventually recognize that we want to be someone different. I evolved from being a sinner burdened with guilt, shame, and unworthiness to being a soul who is simply making different choices, some good and some bad, and it is in the act of making these choices that I define who I am.

God cannot love us unconditionally and "judge" us as bad at the same time. God can give us free will and allow us to experience the inevitable negative consequences of our harmful choices, however, and perhaps those karmic consequences may be misperceived as judgment.

To heal our spiritual negatives is to choose a higher path. We acknowledge our negative choice, we feel the impact of that choice, and we make any appropriate amends. Then we choose to be something better and live that higher choice from that moment on.

I know that this spiritual perspective of sin and forgiveness could be seen as a radical shift from Christian religious teachings, but it is a shift only in how our negative choices are conceptualized. I also recognize that because our poor choices may deeply hurt another, we may tend to feel the need to punish and belittle ourselves by designating ourselves as sinners. I feel that God wants us to discard this misconception of our essence. No one is without negative choices, and still each of us is of God and with God always. God loves us no matter what choices we make.

Joining Hands

For a few months after my spiritual experience, I struggled with how my Christian religious beliefs and foundation meshed with this newly found spiritual path I was headed down. Although I was comfortable with this path, knowing that Jesus had given it to me, it felt different and almost segregated from religion. I saw myself on a journey that pushed the edge of the envelope in effect, a journey that many traditional religious people would find foreign and beyond comfort, maybe even frightening. Initially, I determined that there were two glorious paths, separate from each other, but parallel in their destination of Heaven. This categorization arose solely from my need to assimilate what was transpiring, not from any awareness or knowledge given to me. I think that because the shift in my focus was so dramatic and instantaneous, the contrasts between religion and spirituality were highlighted. Without the benefit of a gradual transition, I suddenly felt like an outsider in my own church community.

For several months now, I have participated in two groups that focus on God: a Bible study and a spiritual group. These two venues address our relationship with God and the universe via different approaches: one is Christian based and the other is more mystical and cross-religion based. At first I saw myself as an interloper in both groups because I did not fit squarely into either. I felt unsure as to whether there was any religious sect or philosophy with which I would wholly identify. But as I continued, I saw the beauty in these coinciding bookend experiences. I recognized that they did not inherently oppose or contradict each other, but that they were merely different interpretations of the same God. Now I see myself as coming full circle and not only belonging to both of these groups, but also belonging to all. Now, instead of focusing on our differences and feeling threatened by them, I seek to learn and grow from others' experiences and beliefs that are unique from mine. And I see, feel, and respect the beauty in every person's chosen path.

I think I am finally at a place where I am not concerned with aligning spirituality and religion, or finding a group that matches my beliefs, or labeling myself to help others identify me or even for me to identify myself. If someone asks me if I am religious, I say that I am. If someone asks me if I am spiritual, I say that I am. I am both, yet I am more. I Am.

The problem with labeling ourselves is that it can be limiting. When we use the words "religious" and "spiritual," we are impressed with specific, confined connotations uniquely defined by our experiences. Labeling can result in miscommunication, because many of us define words differently, and it can cause us to resist connecting with each other, because it highlights our differences. My preference now is to recognize our commonality: we are spiritual beings seeking God and God's truth. A better description might be that we are spirits experiencing God.

Whether you label yourself as religious or spiritual, for lack of better terminology, you should experience God with your eyes and heart open. This involves your conscious act and intent of openly accepting all of God, without the stigma of societal or religious boundaries. Think and reason for yourself with God's guidance. Question hard-and-fast rules, particularly religious rules that have no exceptions. Question exclusive paths to Heaven. Thoughtfully consider others' beliefs, research different religions, talk to people about their experiences of God, and allow your relationship with God to broaden and define itself.

Try to recognize when you've gone beyond considering others' beliefs to the point where you are relying on others' convictions, because then you have let fear or insecurity diminish your trust in yourself. Simply accepting the beliefs of your parents, your friends, or your spouse or mate may appear to be the easy or acceptable course of action, but in doing that you put a middleman between you and God. You've effectively given God someone else's phone number. In making a conscious decision to grow up spiritually, you could discover and solidify your own beliefs and let God know that you have your own direct number to communicate.

Signs in your life will tell you the difference between an honest and open relationship with God and a fearful adoption of others' beliefs. When you feel the irrepressible wave of love for God and your fellow human beings, then you will know that you have an authentic relationship with God. When you are filled with gratitude for the blessings and opportunities your life provides, you will have no doubt that you are truly experiencing God.

Although I wholly believe that God wants us to trust ourselves first, please understand that I am not advocating, in any manner, a free-for-all where we justify our actions because that's just what we wanted to do. I am advocating that we bring our decisions, beliefs, and ultimately our lives to God and then follow God's direction. God will protect us and lead us down the right path if we go inside and listen to Her.

We must go inside, for God does not speak to us with words or a voice that we hear with our ears. Her voice is far more subtle. God communicates to our hearts or intuition by giving us a sense of knowing that rings true to our core. The subtlety of God's voice may frustrate us at times, yet there is great beauty in Her messages, as they are not limited by human language. Through feelings, we experience the purest form of communication, and, more powerful than hearing the message, we *feel* the message. Yet we seekers of black-and-white, tangible, and solid interactions tend to dismiss the touchy-feely methods of God and Her world.

If we stop dismissing what our mind suggests is not real, we will begin to notice the coincidences that aren't coincidences, the whisper of a voice from within, the thought to call someone at the most opportune time, the "ah ha" moment that sends chills through our body . . . . Trey and I have been led to incredible places when we have given credence to those moments. So the first step in our pursuit of hearing God is to trust our own heart and instincts that are grounded in love and honesty. Our distrust of our own feelings and intuition, our insecurity about our ability to hear God, and our fear of missing the boat to Heaven, lead us to look for the answers outside of ourselves instead of within.

I recall an *Oprah* show in which during her "Remembering Your Spirit" segment, a woman in the audience expressed her genuine discomfort with the idea that God is within and not separate from us. I don't remember her specific words, but they were to the effect that she could not make that leap, as God to her was so great and awesome that to believe that God is within us was disrespectful and inconceivable. She saw God as big and humans as small, and it disturbed her that we dare consider ourselves as being godly.

I admit that a paradox exists: to say we are God is both true and false. We are not all-knowing or all-powerful or all-loving, so we are not God—and yet we are, as our essence is God's love. When we acknowledge that we are made of God's love and that God resides within us, we are not declaring that we are equal with God, but we are declaring that we are aligned with God. When God says He created us in His image, He is telling us that the spark of our existence, being, and essence is Him. He wishes for us to be aware of our godly essence so that we may recognize our own greatness and potential and grow in our relationship with Him and each other.

By now it is apparent that I have chosen generally to forgo footnoting or cross-referencing this book with biblical references. I feel that tying my experience directly to the Bible would limit the focus of spirituality, almost defining it as an exclusively Christian experience, which it is not. I am striving not to miss the forest for the trees. God inspired the Bible to help us grow closer to Him, and humans have organized religions for the same purpose. As I expressed previously, our holy texts and religions are not the end but rather a means to the end. The "end" or goal is our enhanced personal relationship with God. We are free to choose religion to assist us to that end, and we are free not to choose it.

I feel it is important here to acknowledge my gratitude toward organized religion, Catholicism in particular. I began my search for God and Jesus by attending the Catholic church. I needed a venue to focus on God, and the Catholic church openly welcomed me, educated me, and shared with me the strength of its faith and beliefs. Catholicism served as a beautiful means to achieving my existing relationship with God.

I have struggled with the fact of having had a personal encounter with Jesus, knowing wholly that Jesus is real, alive, and God's son, yet not feeling compelled to preach about Jesus or convert non-Christians to Christianity. Logically, I of all people should be seeking others to accept Jesus as their savior. But Jesus has not compelled me to follow that seemingly rational path. Instead, I see Jesus in a light that I was unable to see Him in before. Jesus came to this earth to help the lost souls, the lost sheep, who could not find their way to God and the truths of God on their own. He lived a life of truth, a life of love, so that all who lived after Him could look to Him and His life to see God's truth illuminated. Yet many souls in the past, now, and in the future have seen, do see, and will see the truth of God without a relationship with Jesus. And Jesus rejoices in their knowledge, discovery, and remembering. So even knowing that Jesus' life was God on earth showing us the way, I understand that Jesus wants us to seek and know the truth, and that it doesn't matter to Him whether it is through a direct relationship with Him, or with His (our) Father.

As I focus on my spirituality, what I wish is for others to trust in their own spiritual nature and to possess the joy and peace that I now have. But if you choose not to open the door to the spirituality that I have experienced, you are not wrong or lost. Each person's relationship with God is unique and personal. How you choose to strengthen that relationship is just as unique. Your relationship with God must fit within the guidelines of your own heart and comfort. It only matters that you are focused on God and are bringing more love and goodness into your heart and life. As with any relationship, you will find that your relationship with God is not static. Over time it will change and grow, it will evolve and deepen. When you allow that to happen, the beauty will amaze you.

So I am not advocating that "my way is the only right way." Some of my family members, who feel no connection to my experience, initially felt that I might try to "convert" them to this "new religion" I had discovered. Spirituality is not a religion but an awareness that embraces our inherent interrelationship and interconnectedness with God, every existing soul, whether on this plane or another, and the world in which we live. And sharing my experience is not about conversion, nor is it anything new. My hope is to present the tremendous potential that God's presence can have in our lives. The last effect I want to create is anxiety because you feel you don't get it or aren't connected to it. Opening the door to God is a process. Each step in the process will happen when you are ready. There are no time restrictions, nor are there prescribed rules or actions to follow to get you there. No judgments are attached, and no comparisons to others are made. Each relationship with God is individual and beautiful in its own way. When you are ready to be more connected to the workings of God and Her world, pray to discover and strengthen that connection. Be patient. And then experience God's truth resonating within you.

I hope that in realizing that we all come from God and that each relationship with God is unique, we will be tolerant and nonjudgmental of others' paths to God. For instance, attending church every Sunday strengthens some people's relationship with God. For others, church attendance is not necessary. We all know that the physical act of going to church does not itself make a relationship with God. Our relationship with God is within ourselves at all times, whether we're at church or elsewhere. So why should we judge others, or ourselves, by irrelevant factors such as how often we go to church or which church we attend? These are but two of a multitude of examples of how our society judges whether we are religious or not. My advice is not to entangle yourself in the wrong game by focusing on meaningless standards. Use church, use the Bible (or Torah, Koran, etc.), use your relationships with others, use your experiences, and use life to grow with God.

You may have come across the acronym WWJD, which stands for "What would Jesus do?" This is a beautiful question, one by which we could strive to lead our lives. For non-Christians, the equivalent acronym would be WWLD, that is, "What would love do?" Love and Jesus are one and the same. The highest path to choose is love. Whether we consider ourselves religious or spiritual, and even if we are in the process of discovering our relationship with God, let us join hands and recognize that God = love, the common thread that weaves us all together.

The Faces Of God

In seeking a deeper relationship with God, I have found it helpful to identify the different roles God plays in our lives. I came across one thought-provoking analysis of these roles in a family values class at our church in Dallas. Of course, God is so much more than these roles because He is everything. I am attempting not to categorize God, but to suggest some of the ways that God relates with us and we with Him. As you consider these roles, keep in mind that you are God's love. You can very literally empower yourself with this knowledge.

ege *God as creator*. God is the ultimate creator and we are co-creators with Him. Creation is an infinitely ongoing process. God answers our prayers creatively, we solve problems creatively, and we re-create ourselves every moment by our decisions. At times I have felt ecstatic about the way our creativity links us so strongly and directly with God.

Our creative abilities, which are given to us by God, provide such a glorious opportunity for us to receive God. For instance, in our artistic creative endeavors, whether they be painting, writing, sewing, gardening, dancing, playing music, playing with children, or any other endeavor, we can unleash beauty that we didn't know we possessed. We clear our minds, we clear our hearts, and we open ourselves to create by inspiration. We open and free ourselves, enabling God to create through us. All we need do is look at a great painting or listen to a great musical composition, and we can see or hear God's inspiration and creativity at work.

I believe that everyone has creative gifts. Some people may be reluctant to pursue their talent because they put unrealistic expectations on themselves. Others may not even be aware of their creative outlets. I discovered my passion for writing in my thirties. The way I feel when I write is almost indescribable. I feel more alive: I am energized, amazed, joyous, peaceful, connected, all in one. I feel a sense of purpose, knowing that my passion stems from God and love and that I am giving to myself by giving of myself.

Now that I better understand our creative nature, I recognize that our creativity is at work not only in our artistic endeavors, but also in every aspect of our lives: our careers (science, education, business, medicine, law . . .), our personal lives, raising our children—everything. When we recognize our creative nature, we begin to truly understand the control and power we have over our lives. And when we access our creative power by turning within, that is, by looking to our spirit or inner self, we are opening the door for God's creativity to inspire us.

We readily acknowledge that our actions and words can have significant impact on others; however, we often speak and act without considering that impact. With a kind word or gesture, we can create love and peace for another. With impatience or criticism, we can create negative emotions in others. When we are mindful that everything we say and do is creative and can and will impact others as well as ourselves, then we become more careful, respectful, and loving in all that we do.

Our creative ability extends beyond our words and actions and even applies to our thoughts. I know that for many of us this is a more difficult concept to grasp, but be mindful that our thoughts are creative, and see if it begins to ring true. Our intent is the catalyst that steers and molds our creations. Our intent is also the energy that the universe "reads" or receives to assist us. Our thoughts and desires are as directly linked to intent as our speech and behavior are.

⁕ *God as caller.* God is always calling for a relationship with us. But we are not always listening. I read a study that said spouses average four minutes of direct conversation a day. It was referring to quality conversation, when you look each other in the eye and give all of your attention to the other. Four minutes! This seemed so ridiculous. Then I looked at my own life and the demands of family, and I realized that some days go by when I don't take five minutes to connect with my husband—or myself—or God. On those days, it is like I chose the "chaos in life" tape, stuck it in the cassette player, put on the headphones, and muted out everything else, including God.

It is easy to do. Our daily demands are imminent and glaring and much, much louder than God. I find that I usually slip into that mode without realizing it. When I finally do recognize what I've done, I remove the headphones and see that I can deal with life and open up to God at the same time. In fact, answering God's call helps me to deal with life even better.

A great way to listen to God is through meditation. Meditation seems to be a familiar, if not common, practice in our country today. It can mean nothing more than setting aside a quiet, reflective time when we clear our heads of the daily demands of life and allow our inner thoughts and feelings to surface.

When I began my meditative practices, I found myself burdened by the questions of "How often?" "How to?" and "How long?" Such self-imposed regulation pushed me away from meditation rather than drawing me into it. Now I have released those concerns and enjoy five minutes here or thirty minutes there. Daily practices are nice but not always realistic. We should use meditation to bring peace to our souls, not stress. Having experienced the peacefulness of those quiet moments over the years, I am better able to tap into that tranquil solitude when I find myself sucked into the whirlwind of daily life. I merely take a few minutes to go inside and center myself again with God and love.

My prayer time and my walks in nature are also times when I go inside. Find what awakens your spirit and use it when you need assistance to reconnect with yourself. You could use nature, music, the flicker of candlelight, exercise, the smell of incense, journaling, or even a warm bubble bath. Pamper your spirit, nurture your spirit, tend to your spirit so that you easily recognize it. In the place that you find your spirit, you will find God.

I love the following anecdote that one of our priests once shared: Ms. Smith goes over to Ms. Baker's house every day for tea. Ms. Smith talks and talks and then always leaves before allowing Ms. Baker to speak. Despite years of this routine, no friendship ever develops between the two because Ms. Smith never stays to listen to Ms. Baker. It is the same with our relationship with God. We can pray and talk to God all we want, but if we never listen to Her, our relationship will not grow.

God as deliverer. God is constantly delivering us to new and better places, whether by answering our prayers, directing and guiding us, or bringing His workings to us. We may realize God's delivery long after it's done, as it is happening, or not at all.

Early in my relationship with God, I was able to see His answers only with the passage of time and the benefit of hindsight, as when He sent John to me. As my relationship with God deepened, I became aware of His signs in my life as they occurred, as when He led me to creative writing.

God may answer our prayers in different forms than we expect, so we must look to the essence of what we desire and then let it unfold. Let God decide what is good for us. As previously stated, we often form expectations based on what our *mind thinks* we need, not what our soul needs.

When I pray to God, I do not place parameters of time or direction on His delivery; instead, I release my need to God, knowing that He will answer when and how it is best for me. Often I get a sense relatively quickly where He is leading me or that my prayer is not one that needs to be addressed now. Our ability to listen to God and to recognize His signs grows as we grow with Him. That is how my family ended up in Colorado. Neither Trey nor I was praying for a change, but we both sensed God leading us to the opportunities here. And still, I know that God is far more involved in my life than I can even begin to see.

When we wholly give our will to God, we allow God to work in our lives in ways that span farther than what we imagine as possible. We are effectively saying, "Wherever you take me or deliver me, I will go."

Erin has experienced this in her life. After almost dying from a cancer treatment, she gave her will to God. Since that time, God has worked in Erin's life in dramatic ways by sharing her inspiration in many venues: first a newspaper article, then a radio broadcast, next a slot on *20/20*, and, finally, exposure on *Oprah*. Although neither Erin nor her husband, Doug, sought these media appearances, they both acknowledge that God is responsible for them.

The effectiveness of God's delivery is dependent on how much of our control we set aside. Let's face it, many of us are control freaks. Our efforts to maintain control are effectively busy signals when God calls. We're not willing, so don't bother. I know that relinquishing control is scary. But our frame of reference is that of our earthly relationships, in which it does benefit us to develop our own control and not allow another person to dominate us. However, our relationship with God is a completely different matter. God is All: all-knowing (omniscient), all-powerful (omnipotent), and all-loving. Without reservation, I recognize that my life will be much greater under God's control than under my own limited control, which doesn't possess even one "omni"-positive quality.

⁂ *God as covenant maker*. God is creator, caller, and deliverer all in one, and hopes for something from us in return. Our relationship is a give and take. I'm not suggesting that God punishes us for failing to live up to our end of the deal, but He hopes that we will respond to Him by helping ourselves and others. In religious terms, God wants us to witness our faith and live by His commandments; in spiritual terms, God wants us to live through our spirits, that is, from the inside out. At the core, He wishes for us to live a life of love.

Giving our will to God exemplifies this "deal-making" relationship with God. We relinquish our paths of control, and God receives our willingness to go down His path. He is then able to navigate where, how, and when we are to do His work. In return, we receive His glorious gifts. We find ourselves thrilled to be alive, in love with our life, because we are filled with a heightened experience of peace, joy, and beauty. Our spirits shed their fear and are fulfilled living out their purpose of sharing the light of God's truth and love. It's a win-win deal.

Although there is reciprocity in our relationship with God, we must be mindful not to "test" God. When we require that God satisfy our specific demands, we are not turning to God, but rather testing Him by qualifying our faith. Thankfully, God does not play our immature spiritual games. God simply promises us that if we turn to Him, He will answer. Demanding specific acts from God is a red flag that we have clung to fear and insecurity and have not given ourselves to God. Only when we release our control and expectations and truly trust God, can God exercise His part of the bargain and answer in harmony with our highest good.

Sharing God With Our Children

Here are some ideas to consider that might help us teach our kids about God. As with values and morals, children should first learn about God at home. Values, morals, religion, and spirituality can be reinforced at school and church, but parents, or caretakers, must lay their foundations.

When my children were very young, I was insecure in my ability to teach them about God because I had never read the Bible in full. I did not know well the participants or scriptures of our religious history, so I felt inadequate to teach my kids. Now I see how ludicrous my thinking was. I had a real relationship with God that I could share with them! Here's how we now share God with our children:

- Sometimes, after our children pray (either "Our Father" or "Now I Lay Me Down to Sleep"), Trey or I say our prayers out loud. This allows them to hear how we talk to God, like a normal conversation. They hear our concerns for our family and for others. They witness our love for others, our gratitude for the blessings in our lives, and what we find truly of value in life.

- We share examples with them of times when we were aware that God answered our prayers.
- We *attempt* to explain how God talks to us (which makes for some interesting conversations, as you might imagine!).
- We ask our children if they hear God talking to them. Our kids have shared some of their dreams about God and Jesus that we probably wouldn't have learned about otherwise.
- We tell them that God loves them forever and no matter what they do, in addition to our loving them. This can provide a safety net in effect, because parents make mistakes, but God doesn't, and His love is unconditional.
- From Erin we adopted the idea of a prayer candle gathering. From time to time before bed, we sit in a circle, light a candle in the middle of the circle, and turn out the lights. We then each take turns thanking God for the things we're grateful for since the last prayer candle. You can learn a lot about your children and what's important to them in this forum.
- We read from a children's or beginner's Bible. Even if you don't have kids, I recommend this if you are intimidated by the Bible. It's like having *Cliff Notes*! I've learned a great deal from these Bibles because they hit the highlights and simplify.
- We point out God where we see God, whether it be in a rainbow, a sunset, another person, or them.
- When we hear or think of something we want to pray about, we do it right then, out loud with them.
- Although we have not yet done this because our kids seem incapable of sitting still for more than a few moments, I think that it would be beneficial to have them participate in our

meditative or quiet times so that such practice becomes a part of their normal routine in life.

The souls of children can be so pure, open, and innocent. Children have a natural connection and closeness to God that they accept without doubt or critical analysis. For some reason, as we age and mature, we lose our open hearts and have faith only in those things that we can see and touch. Let us nurture our children's openness. Seize the opportunity to encourage them to trust their hearts and to build a solid and lasting foundation with God. If we don't reinforce their openness, the world will strip it from them and soon they will be where we are, searching to rediscover what we once knew.

SIXTEEN

Looking Closer at Ourselves

Reflecting On Age

Trey and I had what I consider the perfect date recently. We hiked to the top of a mountain that overlooks our town and is a local landmark. Then we went to a popular Mexican food restaurant for good food and a margarita. This restaurant is frequented by the college crowd, and they were out in full force that evening. I casually observed these young adults and reminisced about that phase of my life, roughly fifteen years ago, with a nine-year marriage and three kids richly filling the time since. I watched a boy walk up to a table of four girls. It took only a few minutes of more frequent glances and bigger smiles to know which girl he had his sights on. Trey agreed with my comment that it is great to be out of the stage of life in which physical looks are the first and primary method of judging and being judged.

On the one hand, my distance from the superficiality of first appearances comforted me. On the other hand, I had to acknowledge that I had reached the point in my life where I am both seeing and feeling the effects of aging. Wrinkles are beginning to carve my face, my body is less firm and flexible, injuries take longer to heal, my eyes and teeth require significantly more maintenance, and of course, there are other consequences. I find it ironic that although I knew intellectually that someday I would see the signs of aging, I am shocked that they have actually begun to appear.

I have friends in their forties and friends in their twenties, and socially I relate to both sets equally. Yet I made a completely innocent statement to some friends recently that made me realize that I identify more with the younger set. We were in my favorite Mexican restaurant in Dallas, partaking again of great food and margaritas. I was telling my friends all about my experiences in Colorado for the nine months that I had lived there. I was commenting on how dry the weather is in Colorado, so dry in fact that in ten years I'll probably *look like* I'm fifty. Well, in ten years I will actually *be* forty-seven! Reality check! Why is it that I identify with a twenty-five year old and not a fifty year old? Maybe it's because I've experienced my twenties, so I'm still able to relate to that crowd, and I've yet to experience my forties and fifties. But I believe that is only part of the explanation. The disparity in my perspective lies in the deeper conflict that I feel between my spirit and my body. My spirit and mind are growing and expanding. My life is doing the same. How can it be that my body is on the backslide while the rest of me, the essence of me, is moving forward?

I didn't intend to get into this midlife crisis stuff, but since I arrived here, both figuratively and literally, I'll complete this line of thought. To me, forty is what thirty was to my parents' generation. We can account for the decade jump because we are both living longer and starting marriages and families at a later age. Fortyish is a time of reflection, but more significantly, a time when our awareness kicks in that time is running out. (Some would even argue that time speeds up during the second half of life.) It doesn't seem to make a big difference whether you are content or discontent with your life—there seems to be an inherent longing for all that is left to accomplish.

When I begin to feel the anxiety of approaching midlife, I turn to one thought—Erin. First, I think about what she would give to live to forty. The alternative to not growing old is dying. With that awareness, I acknowledge the gift of every day, of life, and of growing old. So I intend to celebrate my fortieth with fervor and gratitude rather than lament and depression. Second, I think about how Erin has lived, learned, and contributed to this world in a mere thirty-six years as if she has lived many more years. My aim is not to try to mirror Erin's accomplishments, but to follow her model of *how* she has accomplished such a rich life. And that is through her focus on God = love. In her nearly five years of living with the disease that will kill her, Erin has sifted through the falsities and illusions of life and has found the purpose and meaning of life in her spiritual journey: simply allowing God's love to flow through her. That lesson is her gift to us. I don't know when or if I will reach the point where I see the beauty, purpose, and gift in every moment as Erin does, but I am profoundly more grateful for life because of God's messages to me through Erin.

Our Bodies

I sense that here is the appropriate place to turn the discussion to our bodies. I know that this topic is important to address because the first "sin" I confessed to Jesus was disliking my body. I have come far in cleansing this negative, although I admit that it took a longer time than I expected and that I still have moments of relapse when I have to return my focus to the spiritual purpose of my body. I have found that God and His helpers typically do not answer our questions and concerns outright, but rather help us to discover the answers ourselves. I think it will be beneficial to share the process of my cleansing, which illustrates the answer God has helped me to see.

First I want to share an observation of my husband's. Trey feels that people who know me or see me will not be very sympathetic to this discussion because by most standards my body is attractive. And I acknowledge that he is right on both counts. But the essence of this discussion is not about whether I have a good body or not, that is, this is not a personal issue. I feel that God is using me to help all of us focus on the spiritual purpose of our bodies.

The first step I took toward cleansing was to conceptualize exactly what negatives I clung to with respect to my body. I decided to reexamine the moments I focused on my body during my encounter with Jesus and remember what my corresponding thoughts, awarenesses, or feelings were. Looking back at that experience, I saw four specific times when my body was the focal point.

The first occurred soon after I arrived in Jesus' presence. I saw my body from above, and my body's imperfections seemed exaggerated. My body had been positioned so that it was completely open and bare. Then Jesus gave me my first pure consciousness, and that was the awareness of my nakedness. I was ashamed and embarrassed and desperately wanted to cover myself, but He wouldn't let me. Instead, Jesus comforted me with His message. He said my shame and embarrassment did not derive from my own fault, but rather from Adam and Eve's original sin.

I now have a broader understanding of Jesus' message of original sin. The symbolism of Eve partaking from the Tree of Knowledge is that, collectively, our spirits chose to know everything and experience everything, good and bad. In order to know all, good and bad, we removed ourselves from the solely positive, peaceful, loving, and harmonious environment of God's spiritual world. God allows us to know all, through our human experiences. *So there is no fault in my shame, but rather a choice to know shame.* I felt shame and embarrassment, not because I did something wrong, but because I chose knowledge; my shame is a consequence of that choice, an experience that I chose to know. We allow ourselves to be misdirected by man's labeling of Eve's choice as sinful. We must remove the negative connotation from "original sin" to understand that God is honoring our choice, not punishing us. It is intriguing that my first pure consciousness with Jesus was awareness of my nakedness, the same first experience of Adam and Eve upon choosing knowledge. Jesus was allowing my spirit to re-experience my choice to know all, which is the reason for, and the birth of, my human experience. It is extraordinary to have been given that experience again.

The second focus occurred during my pure state of confession, when I confessed to disliking my body. Upon reflection after the experience, I was surprised by that confession because I had never before considered my dislike as wrong or harmful to me.

My third focus occurred during my pure state of remorse. During that time, I was consumed by the pain of not being perfect like Jesus, *for Jesus*, both in *body* and soul.

Jesus addressed my pain when He forgave me and made me pure by giving me the knowledge that I could not be perfect. He relayed that I should strive for perfection yet accept my shortcomings without guilt.

The fourth and final focus occurred after my pure states were over and my conscious thought returned to me. I noticed that my body was dripping on the floor, and I inquired about sex. I acknowledged that I saw sex as bad or wrong, and I wanted to know if my view was accurate. He responded with "Enjoy, enjoy."

Upon reviewing my encounter with Jesus, I more clearly saw two negatives that I had attached to my body: 1) a feeling of imperfection, and 2) guilt and shame because of my mindset that sex is dirty. I also realized that in my encounter with Jesus, He had actually given me answers to remove those negatives. I wasn't able to fully see and use His answers, however, until I pinpointed and fully understood my negatives.

With respect to my body's imperfections, I focused on accepting those that I cannot change. I see it as a matter of control. Although my soul may not be perfect, I possess the control to better myself. I have no control over certain aspects of my body; it is what it is. So I accepted my body with all its imperfections.

Earlier I addressed the more encompassing awareness Jesus gave me on the topic of sex. I realize now, however, that I did not have the same level of focus on changing my mindset toward my body and sex as I did with understanding the other awarenesses that I had received. Barriers do not dissolve on their own but require our effort to change and eliminate them. Cleansing is active, not passive.

The second step I took in my cleansing was to explore why disliking my body would be detrimental to my spiritual growth. I approached this issue by addressing the following questions: What potential or positives am I precluding by my self-imposed negative? What is the essence of my body that God wants me to understand, appreciate, and use?

Now I see our bodies serving three purposes, although my understanding may evolve further over time. Our bodies serve as a shell, a temple, and a vehicle.

Shell: Our bodies are the physical mass, or cages, that hold our true essence. We err in defining ourselves as our body rather than our spirit; when I identify with my body, I am masking my true essence, which is my spirit or soul. When I look in the mirror now, I see my soul dressed in a "Jenice" costume.

Temple: Our bodies are temples in that they house our spiritual beings, our godliness. By disliking my body, I am committing a wrong against God, as I am telling God that I find His gift of my body unacceptable and, accordingly, am refusing to celebrate and appreciate His gift and Him.

Vehicle: Our bodies are vehicles taking us to experiences that we need and that others need from us. The barriers erected by my dislike prevent me from realizing the full richness of the earthly experiences that God desires for me.

I have truly come to understand my body for the gift and the tool that it is from God. I see myself as my spirit, not my body, and I see my body in its spiritual essence of shell, temple, and vehicle. Implicit in this knowledge is the need to respect, appreciate, and care for my body and not to abuse it.

Since my spiritual week, I have attended to my body in ways I hadn't before, by becoming more physically focused. This attention was also a driving force in my change in mindset. Since college, I had not exercised regularly, nor did I focus on how I was nourishing my body. In recent years, I have started karate, learned how to mountain bike, hiked, snow-skied, and attended kickboxing classes. As I became more physical, my body grew healthier, and I gained a more positive outlook toward it. Although my body looks virtually identical to how it looked before my regular exercising, I now see it with completely different eyes, positive eyes. I am also more mindful of the foods I choose to fuel my body. I buy organic foods when they are convenient, and we eat less meat and more vegetables and fruits. My body feels strong, healthy, and alive, which in turn helps me to feel positive and invigorated.

I now fully appreciate the vehicle aspect of my body. With mountain biking, hiking, and skiing, I am in nature, which brings much pleasure and peace to my soul. And in karate, I am in an environment where I am learning again. We spend the first twenty or so years of our lives educating ourselves, and then we stop. Unless we motivate ourselves, we become stagnant and listless. I have discovered that, for me, learning something new stimulates my enthusiasm and passion for living each day.

I am intrigued by the fact that as I have opened spiritually and identified with myself less as a physical being, I have become more physical. I think that in removing the veils that have disguised my body, mind, and soul, I have a clearer understanding of God's purpose for each of these parts of me. In recognizing the true essence of my body, I more clearly see how to use it and how to foster its growth in alignment with my higher purpose.

Celebrating Ourselves

Different people can look at the same person, say Jane Doe, and see different things. One might see her figure. Others might see her fashion style, the brand of watch she wears, the car she drives, the strength of her personality, or whether she smiles a lot. We each focus on different aspects of people because we are individuals with different values. And our values tend to change with age and maturity.

Who do you see when you look in the mirror? Society's influence in general, whether through the popular media or the influence of friends and family, can lead us to focus on the wrong things. We can get caught up in materialism, or having the perfect body and face, or striving to appear a certain way in order to fit into a certain group, when that appearance is not who we really are. I am not saying that money or looking your best or finding like-minded friends is wrong or a bad focus. But I am suggesting that instead of looking externally for self-worth and security, we should look internally.

When I reached the point in my life that I became aware of my insecurity and of viewing myself through a lens of guilt and unworthiness, I began to build my self-esteem by working on my external self. Although my academic and social successes enhanced my self-esteem, I later realized that embodiments external to our spirit and soul will get us only so far. Later yet, I began to reflect internally and focus on what I then termed the "real me," instead of just the physical me. With this reflection and focus, I gained true self-confidence and worth. Even so, I acknowledge that I will always have more to learn and further to grow.

One valuable lesson that I have learned through my spiritual journey is the importance of celebrating ourselves. We celebrate youth and the accomplishments gained during our childhood, yet when we become adults, our celebrations cease. Instead of acknowledging our greatness, we tend to focus on our shortcomings and imperfections.

A channeling session with High Guide broadened my insight into how we should view and treat ourselves. We were discussing Erin. High

Guide said several times that Erin is great, a great soul. Trey responded that Erin does not celebrate her greatness because she feels she is unworthy to celebrate herself and she does not want to put herself above God. (Erin had expressed this opinion of herself to us on numerous occasions. Although Erin believed that she was God's love, she continued to struggle with acknowledging her own greatness, as many of us do.) High Guide's answer was beautiful and enlightening. He said that because we are all God's love, when we celebrate ourselves, we are celebrating God. It's worth repeating: **Because we are all God's love, we celebrate God when we celebrate ourselves!** This makes so much sense!

Celebrating ourselves is tied to self-awareness, which I discussed previously. Celebrating the positives and good in ourselves is not egotistical or selfish. And being humble doesn't mean we are to deny our greatest self. Self-awareness of our greatness is simply recognizing our true self. As adults, we seem more comfortable acknowledging our limitations than our gifts. Our internal beauty is abundant, yet we hesitate or even refuse to see it. Maybe we are more easily persuaded by society's artificial standards because they are tangible and part of our everyday life. If that is the case, then we are small, at-the-moment thinkers rather than big-picture or higher-purpose thinkers. Are we so weak that we are unable to set our own standards and trust our own instincts? Only when we recognize that we are falling far short of our beautiful potential by succumbing to external influences are we able to redirect our lives with greater purpose and awareness.

Although I am not fully celebrating myself yet, I took an important step down that path when I acknowledged that my goal was not perfection, but rather betterment and growth. My tendency is to be impatient and to want to see the results of my efforts immediately. But growth is not a result that will be accomplished tomorrow or a year from now; growth is a lifetime process. I realize that I need to live my life each day in a way that celebrates life, God, love, and me. If I were to die tomorrow, would I be happy and at peace with my choices today?

That question steers my daily focus. So I often remind myself to see my successes in the journey, not just the final destination.

Looking at our own celebration from a different perspective, we can see additional value. In celebrating ourselves, we invite and attract more greatness into our lives. Before my spiritual experience, I referred to this phenomenon as a "self-fulfilling prophecy." Now I recognize this effect in terms of energy or karma. The desires we focus on and work toward, the universe or universal energy created by God will bring our way. But we have to be careful because the universe does not distinguish between what is good or helpful to us and what is bad or hurtful to us. The universe simply follows our desires and intent, as we are given free will and choice. When we choose positive energy and outcomes, we bring that energy our way. Likewise, empowering our negatives, not by virtue of our awareness of them but rather through our acceptance and continuation of them, brings more negative energy our way. Think about it this way: by pinpointing the exact behavior that we know is great within us, we are more likely to reinforce and repeat that behavior.

I'd like to sidestep a bit here. Remember when I told you about Carl? Carl was the person who lost his job and his wife because of his dishonesty. Sadly, he can serve as an example of a person who expends his energy on negatives rather than positives. Carl is not depressed anymore. In fact, he has created his own reality so that he actually sees himself as the victim of his losses, the losses he brought upon himself through his deceit. In his view, his ex-wife has wronged him, his former employer has wronged him, and some of his friends and family have wronged him. And he has proof, or at least items he considers proof. Carl chronicles in writing every critical word and action against him. Some of the people he is keeping notes on are those who are just trying to give him an honest reflection of what he is doing to himself. Others are those he has hurt, who are responding to him through pain.

Carl is unable to see that the negative responses to him and the negative situations in his life are consequences of his own negative actions. Because so much of his time, energy, and focus is directed toward negatives rather than positives, he causes himself to attach to those negatives. He stews, and grudges grow, and bitterness builds. He is consumed with anger and with the goal of revenge through proving he is smarter and richer and more successful than the rest of us. Carl's choices are an incredibly sad lesson in the power of our intent and focus. Please empower your positives and release your negatives.

Some of us may be at a place where we readily pat ourselves on the back. For those of us who aren't, I have four suggestions. The first one is to journal your own actions, words spoken, and thoughts that you are proud of or that make you feel good about yourself. You could include things as simple as being polite or patient with a rude customer, or sending a card to someone. They could be more significant things such as being honest when it would have been easier to lie, or sacrificing part of your busy day for someone in need, or forgiving someone for something that was difficult to forgive. I recommend that you journal on a frequent, consistent basis initially, until you learn to consciously recognize and acknowledge your own beauty in action.

The second suggestion entails finding a person with whom you can share your views of yourself, both negative and positive. Of course, this person must be someone you can trust, but it could be anyone: spouse, friend, relative, counselor, or preacher. I use my husband. Most of the personal things I shared with him at first were my negative thoughts. In telling those things to him, I both released my focus on them and grew more comfortable with the fact that everyone has negative thoughts occasionally and that I'm not a bad person because of them. As a result, my negative thoughts have diminished over time, and my positive thoughts have increased. Now I share my greatness with him, and he with me, without either of us thinking or feeling that the other is bragging. We are both fortunate to have the other to share our self-awareness, each of us seeing the value and truth behind the sharing.

The third suggestion is to truly rejoice in the celebrations and successes in your life. Celebrate yourself on your birthday. Celebrate the beauty of your marriage on your anniversary. And look beyond annual events for celebration. See the greatness in your friendships, parenting, career, creative endeavors, and healthful eating and exercising. Take joy in your spiritual self by acknowledging and celebrating your spiritual focus, whether through church attendance, Bible study, meditation, prayer, empathy, charitable work, or clearing and cleansing.

And finally, accept the good things that come your way. Don't reject or deny yourself the numerous and varied gifts of life because you feel that you don't deserve them or haven't earned them. Accept them with appreciation and gratitude and enjoy them!

All of these suggestions are steps to our higher celebration that we are love. Understand that in our own celebration we are serving our higher purpose and, thus, serving God. We should celebrate our *whole* selves—spirit, mind, and body—to fully serve ourselves and God.

Before I leave this discussion of celebrating ourselves, I'd like to touch upon a couple of related topics. First, I'd like to share with you the specific ways we celebrated our son and prompted him to recognize and celebrate his own greatness. You might remember that within a few hours after standing before Jesus, I received an image of our son strangling his own personality and essence. Trey and I immediately turned our focus to building him up and empowering him. Thankfully, he responded quickly to our efforts. Of course, different personalities will respond to different stimuli, but I thought the following simple yet successful approaches we implemented might be both helpful and interesting:

- We often played follow the leader, with him as the leader.
- We frequently asked what he was thinking about and then empowered him with positive reinforcement. For example, we'd ask him what his favorite color or flavor was before asking his sister so that he would focus on his own likes and dislikes, giving

them credibility, or we'd ask him how he would like to spend the day and then the whole family would do what he wanted.

- Whenever he did the normal things that draw praise from us such as color a picture or work a puzzle, we took the praise a little further. Previously, I had heard myself saying "Great job" and "Good job" and "Aren't you proud of yourself?" and "You are awesome" too many times a day to count. I realized that my positive reinforcement had become so routine that it wasn't having the effect I intended. Our son would hear the words and move on, never truly absorbing them. So we started something new. Every time he received our praise, we had him lift his arms all the way above his head and say "TA-DA!" He couldn't help but truly celebrate himself with that response. He absorbed the praise.
- We placed him in a preschool different from his sister's so that he wouldn't be in her shadow. It also gave him a school and friends that he could claim all to himself.
- Whenever he spoke to us, we would try to stop what we were doing and really look in his eyes and focus on him.
- We treated him and talked to him as if he were a little older than he was.
- We gave credibility to all of his emotions, especially when he was sad, unsure, or scared. I felt that those insecure emotions surfaced more readily during that time because he was taking the opportunity to discover himself and the changes he was experiencing frightened him at times.

Before long, this kid was often running through our house with arms flying and "ta-das" and "yahoos" bouncing off the walls. You have never seen two parents happier to have a positively energized wild thing performing his celebration ritual with the gusto that only a three-year-old boy can.

And as a second and final note, just as my focus on celebrating myself has evolved since my spiritual awakening, so has my focus on myself in prayer. Before my experience with Jesus, I was uncomfortable praying for myself and I generally refrained from it except for the most meaningful of reasons. I felt that praying for myself was selfish, that I was undeserving of God's awesome attention, and that God imposed some random limit on the prayers He would answer, maybe by number or maybe by significance. With those incorrect and now seemingly absurd assumptions, I was careful to pick and choose the prayers that focused on me. Of course, if they were somehow tied to the benefit of others, I felt more comfortable including them.

I find it hard to believe that I once placed such significant limitations on myself and my relationship with God. Where, when, and how did I come to believe that God would ever desire anything less for us than the things that will better us and our lives and bring us greatness? God wants us not only to desire growth and self-betterment, but also to strive for them. We need God's help to accomplish that. How do we get God's help? Through prayer focused on our own numerous needs, both significant and insignificant. And if we don't ever ask for God's help and direction, then how can we ever expect to see God acting in our lives?

Pray for yourself on every topic for which you need insight or direction. Know that it is God's desire for you to focus on yourself, just as it is God's desire for you to celebrate yourself. When I compare how rarely I prayed for myself a few years ago to how great a focus I place on myself in prayer now, I have cause to celebrate myself. As my son would say, "TA-DA!"

SEVENTEEN

Evil and Death

EVIL AND DEATH. These two words are not related, yet I have chosen to address them together because they are both subjects that many people prefer to avoid. If you are one of those people, I hope to help you find the comfort and peace to address the subject of death more readily and to more comprehensively consider the role of evil in the world.

Evil

Before my spiritual experience, I avoided the topic of evil because I knew that evil truly exists and I feared its power. I recognize that some of my past idiosyncrasies originated from this fear. Whenever I found myself at home alone, I would keep the TV on low volume so that it felt as if I were not alone. And I was uncomfortable and sometimes even scared at night in the dark. I even had a hard time watching movies with the devil or evil in them. *The Exorcist*, *Angel Heart*, and *The Devil's Advocate* are a few that I have seen that come to mind. I used to worry that any focus on evil, even a passive focus as a spectator of a movie with evil in it, might effectively open a door to evil and make me more susceptible to it.

I now see how my reluctance in the past to examine the true nature, role, and power of evil postponed my spiritual awakening and growth with God. I felt that if I opened myself to God's spiritual world, then I would also be consenting to open myself to evil. Good and bad, God and evil, were a package deal in my mind; an open door to one world was an invitation to both worlds. In my ignorance, or perhaps superstition, I believed that evil would not have a chance at me if I kept my door closed to all other-worldly or mystical experiences. By keeping my door tightly shut, I built what I thought was a wall of protection around myself. In reality, I built a wall of limitation and fear. I know others who forgo greater experiences with God because of similar fears.

One evening a couple of months before my spiritual experience week, I shared my fear of evil with Erin and another spiritually focused friend, Sharon. I told them that at different times in my life, I have sensed the presence of other spirits or beings around me. My reaction to these sensations was always fearful because I didn't know if these spirits were of love or evil. They acknowledged that because of our fear of the unknown, we often jump to the conclusion that other-worldly occurrences in our lives are somehow wrong or evil. We tend to be frightened by events or experiences that we do not understand or that seem out of our control, especially if we do not yet trust our intuition. So they gave me some wonderful advice to enable me to intellectually get past this fear. They suggested that I call upon God's protection, as I knew that with His protection, evil could not reach me. They also said to ask for and visualize God's protection in a form that made me feel the most safe and protected. For instance, some might feel protected by wearing a crucifix, others by asking for God or Jesus to hold their hand, and still others by asking for a protective dome of God's love and light to shield them.

I was always energized with God's love after being with those two souls, as they helped me to tap into God's world of love and goodness that I seemed less able to access on my own. So that same night, with this heightened feeling of God's presence and power, I sat alone in a darkened room and prayed to God to bathe me in His love and light and to hold my hand. And then I invited whatever it was out there that I feared to confront me. Almost two hours went by and nothing happened. Although it may seem anticlimactic, I greatly benefited from this exercise. It was my first step in tearing down my wall of false protection. With the cloak of God's protection, I knew that I was willing to confront the unknown.

My fear of evil has vanished through the process of my awakening. Although I respect the presence and power of evil, I do not fear it, for I now understand my power over it. Good and evil are polar opposites, but they are not equal in power. Good, or love, will *always* conquer evil. Love disarms evil by stripping it of its power. I also have come to understand how our growth deeper into God's world of love, light, and goodness further distances us from evil. So my "package deal" concept was a misconception precipitated by my fear of the unknown. Asking God for a deeper connection with Him and His world brings you exactly that, closer to God.

A friend of mine from high school, the very one who helped me to try out a faith in God, told me about an encounter he had with evil. He said that for a time he had been asking evil to come into his presence. My response was "Why in the world would you do that?" His answer was that he wanted to come face-to-face with evil and then denounce it. I thought he was crazy. At that time, I couldn't imagine summoning evil to myself. Anyway, he said his wish came to fruition. One night while in his bed, he felt evil present in his room. He denounced it and sent it away.

Although I'm not suggesting that you summon evil as my friend did, I now have experienced a similar event that has helped me to understand the purpose behind his encounter. Shortly after my encounter with Jesus, I was in our study writing about my experience. It was late at night, and all of a sudden I had a sinking feeling. I stopped my writing and felt the heaviness and discomfort of evil. Ever since my encounter, I had been sensing that through the process of my awakening, it would be beneficial, or maybe necessary, for me to confront evil and reject it. By doing so, I would trust both my recognition of evil and my power over it. So I sat on a couch, closed my eyes, prayed for God's protection as I had done before, and told evil to stand before me. I felt its presence more strongly, although I never saw anything. With my whole intent and desire, I denounced evil, rejecting it and its power over me and my family. I instructed evil to stay away from me and my family. I used every disenabling directive that I could think of to make my intentions completely clear. And then the heaviness was gone. I was alone with God and I thanked Her for Her protection. I then knew with certainty that armed with God's love, I not only was protected from evil but could also disempower it.

I still prefer to distance myself from needless and voluntary exposure to evil. Although I know that evil is a matter of choice and cannot take you unwillingly, I feel that prolonged exposure to any negative influence, whether it be violence, exploitive sex, or harm intentionally inflicted upon another for personal gain, can weaken a soul. Such negative influences can harden our hearts and lead us to a false reality in which such things are acceptable. Sometimes, such negatives are even glamorized. I am saddened by the lack of moral responsibility in our music, TV, and movie industries. Not only do these media reach mass markets, but their influence on young, susceptible minds can be devastating. As I have said before, those things that we put our intent and focus on, we bring to ourselves. I hope you see the beauty in surrounding yourself with beauty.

Death

For some, discussing death may be disturbing. Before my brother's death, I was uncomfortable with the topic, but not because I thought focusing on it would bring it to me as with evil. I did not possess a sense of peace with death, so focusing on it just made me terribly sad and uneasy. Craig's death forced me to address it, and now I accept death for its true essence, which is a natural part of the cycle of life.

We all are going to die. You know that, I know that, but not all of us truly accept it. We may even be shocked when it happens to someone we know. How can it be? Your mother is going to die, your father is going to die, your brothers and sisters are going to die, your best friend, your husband, and your children are all going to die. And of course, you and I are also going to die. And not a one of us knows for sure when this inevitable fact of life will transpire.

If we accept this unavoidable truth today, we enhance our chances for a greater life tomorrow and every day after. Living our lives with the awareness that we could die at any time, be it tomorrow or a year from now, motivates us to lead a better life now and to make the most of each day that is given to us. We search for the meaning of life. We treat our relationships with God and others with more care and attention. We express our love more readily, recognizing the risk of the lost opportunity. Rather than wasting significant portions of our lives, we direct our lives with purpose. Rather than taking our lives for granted, we appreciate God's gift of opportunity.

An honest, balanced reflection and focus on death is healthy, not morbid. Those who refuse to address their mortality often postpone their focus on God, their spirituality, and their relationships with others until they are older, when death seems more imminent. When we deny our mortality, we are taking a huge gamble. Physical life gives no guarantees other than that it will end. And it may very well end before we are older.

My goal going forward in the experience of my loved ones' deaths is best described by the oxymoron "beautiful pain." The beauty is in the cycle. Death is both an end and a beginning. It is the end of one cycle of life, our present physical existence, and the beginning of a new cycle, our further evolved spiritual existence. And that cycle is like the seasons, repeating itself over and again. Within each season is new and unique beauty and cause for us to rejoice and celebrate.

The pain flows uncontrollably and intensely upon a death, as death brings us what appears to be the greatest loss imaginable and doesn't consider whether we are prepared for it or not. Our world seems to stop for a while, as the rest of the world goes on. Superficial things that burdened us just the day before are no longer significant. For a brief time, we exist at the primal, basal essence of life. Yet from this deepest pain can arise the greatest beauty. When the pain of death or imminent death takes us to the core of our existence, we are able to focus more clearly on what truly matters most: expressing love, being honest, improving relationships, seizing the day.

Mourning and grieving are not thoughts of the mind but emotions of the heart. They are not only natural but necessary for our hearts to heal and grow. We have seen people deny the pain of the loss of a loved one only to have it surface at a later time and usually with a gradual devastation filling the time in between.

The degree of pain and suffering that we experience upon the death of a loved one is dependent upon numerous factors. Some of these factors are:

- the age of the person who died;
- how the person died, such as by natural causes, murder, accident, suicide, or disease;
- the relationship or familial bond with the person who died, that is, parent, sibling, child, grandparent, friend, and so on;
- the status of our relationship when the person died;
- the spiritual state of the person who died; and
- the survivor's spiritual state at the time of the death.

I'd like to share some thoughts about death that have arisen when loved ones in my life have died.

My grandmother died ten months ago. She was in her early eighties and had been in poor health for a few years. She died peacefully in her sleep. If we could pick our own outcome, we would likely pick one similar to hers. She had a long, healthy, and fulfilling life and then died peacefully in her home at an age acceptable to most of us for death to occur. The pain of her loss is grounded in the loss of her companionship and presence in the lives of her loved ones. The pain is real, yet it is lessened by the fullness of her life; we do not have to endure the pain of unfulfilled expectations in addition to the pain of loss.

My grandfather, her husband, took care of her during her years of failing health. Ten months later, he is barely recognizable as the man he was. The only function he is now able to perform on his own is the act of bringing food from his plate to his mouth. He requires assistance for bowel movements, bathing, walking, and turning over in his bed. When I visited him in a nursing home recently, I sensed that he had lost much of his will and motivation to live. I do not know for sure that my grandfather is ready to die, but it is clear that his children find it difficult to accept that he is dying. They continue with his operations and rehabilitation, holding on to a thread of hope that he will be functional again and relieved of his physical suffering. My father and his brothers and sisters are loving people responding to their father's condition with love and empathy. But my grandfather's age and deteriorating physical condition bring to light a pervading mindset of our society: we do not respect an elderly person's will to die. I find it ironic that we will permit an animal to have a peaceful and humane death rather than continue with its grave suffering. Yet with our loved ones, we cling to life at all costs because of our fears, not the fears of the dying. Many elderly people know when they are ready and their time has come. There are cultures that respect and honor this transition in life. But sadly, ours is not one of them.

My brother Craig died when he was twenty-six years old. He was married, but he did not have any children. I was twenty-nine at the time. His death was my first personal encounter with the death of a loved one. Craig's death was unexpected, and it was brutally painful, especially for my parents, as they faced the almost unbearable pain of losing a child. Yet my family pulled together and survived. We shared a common faith in God, and we supported and strengthened one another with love. The pain of his loss will remain with us forever, but the daily suffering is gone. In my experience, the passage of time was a necessary element in my family's healing and my own, but it was not the only element. We confronted the pain, we lived the pain, and we each found our own way to make peace with it. We grieved and, with time, we regained a sense of wholeness again.

The magnitude of our pain stemmed from unfulfilled expectations: Craig was young and had his whole life ahead of him, and parents are not supposed to bury their children. But the reality is that many young people die and many parents outlive their children.

Grieving is a process. It is a process with no guidelines or boundaries or preconceived paths. Trey's greatest gift to me during my grief was the freedom he gave me; he did not place expectations or time limits on my grieving. He let me know that how I felt and what I felt and when I felt it and for how long I felt it were all okay and normal. I remember that a few months after Craig's death, I experienced a mild panic attack because many of my co-workers and friends expected me to be back to normal again, and I wasn't. Trey reminded me not to take on or accept others' expectations. He helped me to see that I was facing Craig's death and dealing with it, and that I was grieving in a healthy manner. I had to let the process be what it was going to be.

An unforeseen consequence of Craig's death is the beauty it eventually brought to my life. Following his death, I fully understood for the first time that life can be short and that I must live each day to the fullest. I began to appreciate the gifts and opportunities that life presents and to expressly share my love of others with them. I experienced the strength and comfort of God's healing grace by rising out of the depths of devastating pain. I then knew that with God's assistance, I could survive anything. And I was no longer uncomfortable with or afraid of the topic of death.

I feel that my spiritual experience has allowed me to see death in its genuine essence. I still have my fearful moments when I consider the death of my loved ones, but the difference now is that I am able to step out of my fear and into peace. I take comfort in knowing that our spirits live on. I appreciate that this life is not our only opportunity to get life right, which eliminates the finality and gravity of our choices in this life. I recognize that the distance from our loved ones who have died before us is only temporary and physical and that we are truly never apart from them at the soul level. And I know that our healing and evolution continue for as long as we need and that we are destined to be with God in His realm of love, light, peace, joy, and beauty.

Earlier in this chapter I expressed that my goal upon the death of a loved one is to experience beautiful pain. Sadly, shortly after writing that passage, I lost a loved one. I have made several references to "Carl" in this book. He is my brother, and he committed suicide one month ago (September 1998). As you can imagine, my family is suffering greatly right now. My siblings and I now have lost two brothers, and my parents have lost two sons. I hesitate in writing this passage, as I do not want to bring my family further despair, but I feel it is important to share with you how my spiritual awakening has changed my life in the face of tragedy.

Carl is really Bruce. He was thirty-six years old when he killed himself. Bruce had a brilliant mind that enabled him to accomplish great things, but it also enabled him to present to the world a different person from what he really was. Few people saw that he was tormented and troubled and that he had made many harmful decisions in his life. When one of his hurtful paths caught up with him, he could not face up to it and so he chose to end his life.

The pain of my family members is compounded by conflict. Not only are they having to deal with his death, but they are also confronted with the issues brought out by a suicide (guilt and anger), as well as the conflict of trying to reconcile the irreconcilable, that is, resolving the Bruce they thought they knew with the Bruce who really was. It is difficult to fully grasp their suffering.

You may have noticed that I am referring to the pain of my family as "their" pain rather than "our" pain. That is because I am at a very different place now. I found myself responding to Bruce's situation and the tragedy of his death from a different place than with Craig's death. This time I experienced it from my perspective as a spirit rather than a human. I almost feel guilty that I am not suffering as they are, but I don't, because my lack of suffering is not for lack of love of Bruce. I hope that my family understands this.

We had a few days' warning of the crisis Bruce was facing before he took his life. When I learned of the crisis, I naturally and instinctively turned to God for strength. I found that I didn't need my family or my husband or my friends, although I appreciated their comfort; I needed only God. I knew that it was likely that Bruce would commit suicide. A year earlier when he lost his job and his wife, he was suicidal. I was there for him, as were other family members, and we tried to help him. We got him professional counseling, and we gave him our love and support. Although he survived that round, he ultimately chose not to help himself or to accept the love and support of his family. He hit bottom, but failed to seize the opportunity to rise above it by making positive changes in his life. As I described earlier, it was through my aid to Bruce that I learned that we can only give our love—we cannot force others to accept it.

Bruce knew that we were with him again this time, but still he pulled away from us. Our love for Bruce and the support we offered him help me not to feel any guilt or responsibility for his death. I also see the reality of what he did: Bruce killed himself. It was his choice, his will, his doing, not ours. Not only do I believe that there is nothing that I or anyone else could have said or done to change his choice, but I also remind myself that "I'm not in it." I refuse to take on his negatives.

During the two days of Bruce's wake and funeral, I witnessed God's beauty all around us. I saw God working. I saw the onset of healing and closure beginning their long paths. I heard God speaking through the priest at the funeral. I saw the compassion and love of my family's friends and the strength of the human spirit in all those affected by Bruce's death. I recognized that Bruce is now at a place where he will be forced to deal with his issues, no longer able to deny them. Although he would have been better served to have dealt with his issues while on earth, he still will have the opportunity to choose God and love, for Jesus Himself said that He would always leave the ninety-nine in the flock to bring home the one lost sheep.

Much of the pain I feel now comes from the pain that my family is enduring. But I am not suffering as they are, for I know that in the end Bruce will endure. I know that wherever he is, he will have the opportunity to begin his healing when he is ready. He will have other lifetimes to deal with the issues he has created. Eventually, he will come to recognize that his essence is love. I accept his life and his decisions as being what he needed for his evolution. I feel that this awareness has lifted me above much of the suffering. I hope that I do not sound cold or callous, for I truly love Bruce and wish that he were still alive. But I know that his death is not the end, but merely a moment in his journey to pure love.

My peace and strength continue as I had hoped they would. My mind thinks that I should be responding differently, as I did when Craig died, but my heart knows otherwise. I am at a spiritual place where I can experience a great loss and feel the intense pain and cry until I have no more tears, and yet experience such pain with a sense of peace and without suffering. With Craig's death, I could not conceive of pain and grief without suffering. Now I have lived it. Maybe it is because I no longer place expectations on this lifetime. Or maybe it is because I have a sense of God's grander plan and understand that we are spiritual beings rather than merely earthly beings. Or maybe it is because, in sharing my life with God, He has shared His supernatural peace with me. No matter the reason, I am able to see God's beauty even in the face of tragedy and I am thankful.

Erin has returned home. She died on October 31, 1998. I am a little raw right now, having lost two loved ones within two months. I will miss her physical presence tremendously. But I am still at peace.

Our friend Sharon was with Erin when she died. I am very grateful for that for many reasons. One is that Sharon's presence always brought Erin much peace, as Sharon is a very peaceful and spiritual person. Another is that Sharon was honored by being able to help Erin in her last hours. And finally, Sharon was willing to share with me the beauty of Erin in her death and transition between the two worlds. This last reason is a great gift to me because I found it very difficult being in Colorado, physically unable to be with Erin (in Dallas), or even say goodbye to her, at the end.

Erin's death was peaceful. She was conscious and lucid through the end, which I know was something she deeply desired. I am so thankful for that. Sharon relayed that Erin continued to share her inspirational love even as she was dying, her final communications being of concern for her loved ones whom she was leaving behind. All who saw her in her last few days say she was both peaceful and radiant in God's love. Can you imagine a body that is literally disintegrating from cancer and the poisons of chemotherapy and radiation actually exuding a radiance? Erin's spirit was shining through. I imagine that witnessing the beauty and love around an almost dead body would be powerful proof that the spirit lives on.

When Doug called to let us know that Erin would die soon, I was pained not to be able to be with her, so I went to her the only way I could. I went to God and to Erin through my spirit. For an hour or more I prayed for Erin, I said my goodbyes, and I sent her imagery to help her in her transition. I sensed that she had battled her cancer with such drive and determination for so long that she was having difficulty releasing the fight. I reminded her that she had completed all of God's work and that she had addressed all of her concerns for her loved ones. It was time for her to be with God and Jesus, her guides and angels, and her loved ones who had predeceased her. And it was time for her to receive the celebration for a job well done. I felt the magnificent brilliance of her spirit, and I sensed the tremendous joy of the spiritual world that arose from her glorious work on earth and its impending reunion with her. I found peace by being with Erin through my spirit.

She was truly a precious gift from God to me and to so many others. You rarely find people with the level and strength of positive qualities that Erin possessed. Because her gift is hard to replace, my human nature began to feel a void when she died. Then my spirit took over. Erin was a window to God. By sharing God within her she gave me the greatest gift possible—she helped me to see God within me. Through this book and personal relationships, I continue the work that Erin helped me begin: I share God within me so that others might see God within themselves. So, despite the pain of her loss, I see that her beauty lives on in me and the multitude of souls she has touched, for her beauty was God's love, an eternal gift.

By our very nature, we are drawn to love as well as to strength and perseverance in the face of an enormous challenge. Erin's cancer was her battle. When we put ourselves in her shoes, most of us feel that we would crumble. But Erin grew in love, strength, and positive focus. Because of her inspiring response, she became a magnet. We yearned to know how and from where this beauty came to be. As a person who lived a life of love, Erin is a testament that each of us can choose a life of love. For those of us who knew her, her greatness raises the bar and challenges us to live better, richer, more glorious lives. Erin was fond of the phrase *carpe diem*. Here are some of the ways I remember Erin seizing each day:

- She allowed God's love to flow through her more freely and purely than most. And she did not hesitate to share with others her connection with God, even before the cancer.
- I can only imagine the magnitude of the daily physical discomfort and pain of living with cancer, chemotherapy, and radiation. Yet Erin literally never complained, and she always had a smile on her face. She walked with more energy and pep in her step than many able-bodied, healthy people. When you visited her with the purpose of brightening her day, you were amazed to find that she had brightened yours; you left energized, positive, and peaceful because she rubbed off on you. Despite having lungs that were riddled with cancer, she could be interviewed without coughing because, according to her, God gave her that strength. Closer to the end, your mind seemed to play tricks on you when you saw her, as your eyes saw the shell of a person, but your heart witnessed the strength and perseverance of her spirit.
- She was a person with incredible drive and determination. She coupled her zeal for accomplishing the things she cared about with an equally powerful positive focus, enabling her to live a rich and full life in thirty-six years.
- She not only saw the best in everyone, but she also had the gift of drawing out the best in people. As a result of this gift, she made instantaneous and close friendships with those who crossed her path because she was able to reach and touch others like no one else.

Evil and Death

❧ While living with cancer, she lived life at its core purpose and helped others to sift through the clutter in their lives to find their own core.

In recent years, I have found myself writing poetry at times when I need to release deep emotion. I would like to share three poems that I wrote over the course of Erin's battle with cancer. The first one I wrote while accompanying Erin to the doctor for a chemotherapy treatment.

Morning sickness; afternoon, evening, and night sickness
Finding the bathroom at every location
It's growing inside of her
What should she name it?
Cancer

Fuzzy head or smooth head
Thin face or steroid face
Sometimes with Junior [chemo travel pack] and sometimes not
But always in a hat; always beautiful

No anger; only constant effort to channel the negative to positive
Determination to live:
   raising a child
   having religions to compare
   being a daughter, wife, and friend
   sharing God's love

I wrote the next poem for her on her 35th birthday. I call it "*A Lesson in Flight from My Beautiful Winged Friend.*"

At first I saw her as a butterfly . . .
   Her physical beauty surpassed only by her beauty within
   Graceful . . . admired . . . unique . . .
   Attracting us all

Then I saw her as an angel . . .
> *God's servant*
> *His guide and protector of lesser mortals*
> *Definitely mine*
> *But also to all who cross her path*
> *Expanding us*
> *Flying us higher*
> *Bridging two worlds*

And now I see her as a dove . . .
> *All goodness encompassed*
> *Whiteness . . . pure and brilliant light*
> *God's love*
> *God Himself*
> *Her gentle coo filling our hearts with peace*

> *As she cuddles us in the love and warmth of her soft feathers, her expansive wings fly so many of us closer to God. And during our travel, she shares with each a single feather as a seed for the budding of our own wings . . . her greatest gift to us all . . . a lesson in flight.*

This final poem I wrote when I found out that Erin's cancer had spread to her liver and I was forced to acknowledge that she probably wouldn't beat it.

Just My Friend

My brother died seven years ago
Sympathy was abundantly forthcoming
For after all, he was my brother
Curiously, I fear that others will not understand my pain now
For after all, Erin is just *my friend*
No blood or marriage relation
Just *my friend*

> *But my heart is crying out!*
> *Just* MY *friend*
> *You understand the possession*
> *You feel it too*
> *For Erin touched* me . . . *reached* me . . . *inspired* me *like no other was able*
> *Erin saw God in* me
> *And there are too many "me's" to count*
>
> *So yes, Erin was* just *my friend*
> *And* just *a window to God and Jesus*
> *And* just *an eternal inspiration to our souls*
> *And* just *a most precious gift from above*
> *Thank you Erin for leaving us with so much more than* just *the pain.*

I am so thankful to God for giving Erin the last year of her life. By all accounts she should have died much earlier, as the cancer had spread to her liver over a year before her death. In her last year, God shared her with millions of people through numerous and varied media exposures all over the world. And Erin published her book, *Living with the End in Mind*, just two months before she died. There is so much to celebrate.

EIGHTEEN

Living an Awakened Life

Friday night before my spiritual awakening week, I had dinner with Erin and Sharon. As I have mentioned before, being with those two women always energized me; we celebrated life and God together. Looking back, I now recognize that they were my spiritual soul-friends. They helped me to tap into God's boundless loving energy even at times when I felt disconnected from God. Upon moving to Colorado, I desperately missed those spiritually energized outings. That particular evening, I shared with them how I felt that every aspect of my life was perfect. I was so grateful to God for all the blessings in my life, and I readily acknowledged that I was at this great place because of my relationship with Him. Yet almost as a passing thought, I also acknowledged that this "perfection" made me feel distant from God. As there was nothing to "fix," I essentially felt as if I were walking side by side with God but not holding His hand. I wasn't worried about the distance because I had experienced highs and lows in my relationship with God before, just as in other relationships. Yet I desired that connected, personal bond with God even in the great times. Even when I needed nothing *from* God, I still needed my relationship *with* God. The point of sharing that evening with you is to contrast where I was, at the time my spiritual adventure began, to where I am now as a result of that gift.

Just two days before the beginning of my spiritual week, I was at a very secure, stable, peaceful, and joyous place in life. I didn't need anything, I wasn't searching for anything, and I wasn't under stress or facing strife in my life, other than the typical day-to-day stresses we all face. I was emotionally, mentally, and spiritually healthy, happy, and satisfied. Trey referred to the stage we were in as being "pregnant with possibilities." Trey's hard work and high ethical standards were beginning to be recognized and respected in the numerous venues in which he gave of himself, our family was healthy and happy, Trey's and my relationship was awesome, and I now had a dream in my life, to sell a movie, which gave us an excitement and energy about life that we hadn't possessed before. In other words, we were at a great place, and the future looked even brighter. We were open to and excited about the potential and possibilities of the fruits of our labors. We both had a sense that we were seeing ourselves at a pre-greatness place. This is a little difficult to explain, but it was as if we were approaching the top of our opportunity bell curve. We had no idea what this opportunity of greatness would be, but we both sensed that it was coming. We also sensed that once we reached the top, our lives would be forever different.

And then we were blessed with this incredibly powerful spiritual experience from God. How could this be? We already felt overwhelmed by all His gifts. And still the floodgates of Heaven opened and showered gifts upon us beyond what we had ever thought possible. Our lives were transformed from what we then considered as perfect and alive with opportunity to what I now view as aware and awakened. This aware and awakened life is the gift that has brought us God's gifts of love, peace, joy, and beauty.

In one sense, we are the same two people, as the core of who we are and what we stand for and believe in is the same. Our friends and family who are uncomfortable with our experience take comfort in the sameness of Jenice and Trey. Yet in another sense, we are different, as we are broadened. We are awakened to the God within us and in every person and creature and thing. We see that there is an impact behind every thought we have, word we speak, and action we take. We see that every person is a spiritual being experiencing a chosen human life. We see our earthly life as an opportunity for growth through the exercise of our free will. We see the spiritual realm at work in every person's life, guiding and directing and loving. We see our purpose in this life and in life itself; we see that we are love on a journey to greater love. We see every soul's purpose as serving God, and when we acknowledge that God is within, we are then able to share and serve God by being a window to God for others.

Two religious aphorisms help capture this transformation in our lives. I had heard these aphorisms throughout my life but never gave them much thought until our awakening. They are "I was blind but now I see" and "The truth will set you free."

I was blind but now I see. The truth has always existed, but I didn't see it. Maybe I wasn't ready, or maybe I didn't want to see it. I don't know the reason. In many ways, I was in a dark room searching for the light of truth. And then one day, God turned on the light for me. When you see the truth, you know it and you feel it in your core, for that is where it lies, in your core. Only when I saw the truth did I recognize my prior blindness.

Originally, I was blind to my essence and my connectedness to God. When I cleared away the veils to expose my true self, I drew the curtains from my window to God. Then I worked at cleansing Jenice, and with that began the shining of my window. Now that the curtains are drawn and the window is clearer, I work on expanding my window.

My spiritual insights are nothing new, except to me. I was amazed to discover a whole culture of awakened people and innumerable books written about spirituality. These people and books were around long before May 10, 1996, but I had not yet opened my eyes and heart to God's messages. When I discovered that all that I have been awakened to by God had already been written about, I wondered why God asked me to write a book about my experience. And then I was given the knowledge that every voice is unique and reaches different people. So my voice joins the multitude of other voices of God in saying "When you are ready, we are here."

In God's gift to me of awakening I see my gift to you, which is the ability to conceptualize and articulate that which we all already know within our being but may be unable to see. I feel that God is helping me to bring to my conscious mind that which we all know subconsciously.

I feel so fortunate that God healed my blindness in such a miraculous encounter. But I also know that we can discover God's truth ourselves. We are born onto a sandy beach with pearls of truth buried throughout. We spend our lives sifting through the sand for the truth. As we grow in experience, we become more adept at locating the pearls. And when our lives are struck by storms, we temporarily stop the sifting to rebuild and regroup. When we are solid again, we find that our filter pores are even bigger, allowing us to extract the non-truth more quickly. Although I still have sand in my life, I feel that the pearls of truth now protrude from the surface, their translucent beauty drawing me to them so that the whole truth can be revealed.

The truth will set you free. God's truth has indeed set me free. I am free to share my experience with the world because the gift of experiencing God and His truth gives me courage and eliminates all doubt and fear. I am free to be honest because the truth serves God and me and the person with whom I'm being honest. I am free to celebrate myself, to be joyous, to be at peace in life with a sense of God's grander scheme, to live my life with purpose, and to release the immaterial aspects of life and strive for love and betterment. I am free to trust my own heart, feelings, intuition, and relationship with God because the truth that God is within has been revealed.

I have been in God's river of love for my whole life, but, until my awakening, I held on tightly to a rock of routine, comfort, societal acceptance, and security. God's truth allowed me to let go of my rock and to let His river of love carry me where it will. I know that I will be bumped and bruised from hitting other rocks along the way, but I am in the current of God's river of love and I am "growing" with the flow. I do not intend to limit myself again by grasping another rock.

I do not want to mislead anyone into thinking that awareness and awakening bring automatic resolutions to your problems or perfection to your imperfect ways. Rather, awareness and awakening reveal the destination to attain and the purpose in reaching that goal, and then empower and free us to strive for it. I admit that I am frustrated when I know exactly where I need to head and find myself not yet able to get there. Although I see the path, sometimes it is difficult for me to get to the path or stay on the path. In losing my blindness, I see more clearly my self-imposed and self-constructed limitations.

My connectedness with God continues to cycle through the highs and lows of a rollercoaster. Yet before my experience, I saw my part in these peaks and valleys as largely passive, the active influence being life's events external to me. Now I see each and every experience, good or bad, and significant or insignificant, as a unique opportunity for me to broaden my relationship with God, as all of these experiences are the reason I am participating in the earth school.

I also recognize that the state of my connectedness depends solely upon me. God is always present, ready, and willing to be close with me, but I check in more at some times and less at others. There is nothing inherently wrong with this cycle, and in fact it is normal in all relationships. The great thing now is that not only are my highs higher, but my lows are higher too. And I know that all I have to do is put some effort into us, that is, God *and me*, to get back to holding His hand again. I have discovered that the times that I neglect myself and my needs are the times that I feel more distant from God. In neglecting myself, I am neglecting the God within. I draw closer to God when reading an inspirational book or listening to inspirational readings on tape, talking with my spiritual soul-friends, praying for assistance, meditating more frequently, and focusing on nature by hiking in the mountains or enjoying the beautiful Colorado sunsets. What makes you feel closer to God?

I used to turn my focus to God more frequently in times of need. Now I am always focused on God. Every morning when I wake up and several times throughout each day, I am consciously aware that I am love, that God is within me, and that I am here to serve God. My heart is continuously open to God's direction and guidance. Even when everything in life is going smoothly, I ask for God's assistance to help me grow in love; to help me be a better mom, wife, friend, and servant of God; and to help me make life even better. There is no finish line for the person I wish to become.

I do not look at the struggles in my life as defining a time period (e.g., 1998 was a bad year because of the death of two loved ones) or as being more or less than my fair share. Life is what it is. And I cherish the power God has given me to make it what I want it to be. That which I can't control, I can still control my response to.

Although I see myself as both a child of God and a servant of God, I also know that I am a partner *with* God. Now I see the reciprocity in our relationship; not only do I need God, but God also needs me. God needs us all to continue our work on our own spiritual growth. Even with the help, guidance, and love of God and His world, it is still necessary for us to take the steps toward our own evolution. God needs me to open myself to Him so that we can have a relationship. God needs me to give Him my will so that He can direct where and how and when I do His work. God needs me to be His messenger.

Drawing on my experiences as an attorney, I know that a partnership, like any business deal, is based on consideration given by both parties. For example, one partner may bring money to the table and the other expertise. Our partnerships with God are based on the mutual consideration of love. That is why giving my will to God was a very different experience than I imagined it would be before my awakening, when I saw the act of giving my will as having a negative impact on my life and my control. The operative words that came to mind were "diminished" and "lessened." Having given my will to God, I can tell you the consequential impact on my life and my control: gain, purpose, greatness, fulfillment, acceptance, growth, empowerment, and direction. If I could reword this action to clarify the reality of its effect, I would change it from "I *gave* my will *to* God" to "I *shared* my will *with* God." And knowing that God's consideration in our partnership is the direct and personal experience of His unconditional love, we can wholly trust that His will for us will bring more positive gifts into our lives.

I lived thirty-five years never contemplating that I would share my will with God. Now my will is common with God's: the spiritual growth of all souls. Of course, God, with His omniscient view, is better equipped to determine exactly how we should work together toward our goal. And the best strategy is for Him to use my strongest skills and/or most passionate interests.

So I was led to write a book about a very personal, life-changing, mountaintop experience. I have vacillated between the awe and incredibility of the experience on the one hand, and my comfort with and acceptance of the naturalness of the experience on the other. At times I have thought "Why me?" yet at other times I have thought "Why not?" From the outset of writing this book, I strongly desired to provide at least a glimpse into the pull of my opposing emotions. I assume that it is easy for others to recognize the remarkable nature of my experience and that the "Why not?" aspect is harder to grasp. In my effort to capture this polarity, I use two different approaches.

The first one is my mental path: Yes, my encounter with God was astonishing. Yet on the other hand, why wouldn't such an experience happen? God, Jesus, angels, and guides exist. So why wouldn't they contact us? Most of us accept that God and His spirits interacted with humanity in the past, so why not now? My experience was both incredible and highly probable. But isn't that how God is? God is everything, and I cannot encompass Him with mere words or even thoughts. And although we cannot fully comprehend the magnitude of God, we are still able to have a real and personal relationship with Him. The paradox is inherent. Therefore, I must accept the opposite ends of the spectrum of possibility and everything between.

The second approach comes as a result of understanding the interplay of the trinity of myself: body, mind, and spirit. The root of the conflict stems from the tug of war between my mind and my spirit. The physical, earthly me that my mind fully grasps remains in awe. The spiritual me is at home. It took the incredible encounter with Jesus to open my eyes and heart so that I saw (remembered) the true spiritual essence of humanity. Upon seeing this, I saw life in a new and broader perspective, as having virtually unlimited potential and possibilities. With my broadened perspective, my spiritual experience was not so incredible after all. In other words, because of the incredible gift of standing before Him, I am now able to see that standing face-to-face with Jesus is not such an incredible thing. I am God's love and light. I am a spiritual being. I am connected to God and His world even though my physical elements, that is, my mind and body, disguise my spiritual essence.

With the passage of time, the ingrained effects of my spiritual experience have brought me a peace that I know I will possess for the remainder of my life. This peace I also wish for you. My peace is based on the gifts I have received, and accepted, from God: understanding and accepting God's love and that I am love and that my journey is to become pure love; knowledge that there is a grander scheme to life giving this life purpose; knowledge that God is always with me and that *I* hold the key to opening the door to my heart and a stronger relationship with Him; knowledge that I am always in the loving care of God's world; and knowledge that in letting go of the rock, I am carried by the current of God's love and will, and that the possibilities and my potential are limitless.

Many of us fear the unknown, causing us to fear change and growth so that we latch on to our rocks of familiarity, security, and control. Perhaps you have seen the movie *Phenomenon*. It did an excellent job of addressing the potential of the human spirit and how we limit ourselves. Realized potential does not come to us, we must go to it.

Opening ourselves to life's possibilities and our own potential is a scary but wondrous thing—scary in that we may feel as if we are setting ourselves up for failure, as well as the criticism of others; wondrous in that we remove the barriers to growth and we invigorate life. Many of us as adults know what our inherent strengths and abilities are, and we tend to stick with challenges that we know we can likely attain. Often it is in our attempts at challenges that are not easily attainable that we begin to see how much greater we truly are. Screenwriting is what initially opened my eyes to my own potential. I didn't know whether I could write a movie, and then I did. The two fruits of this accomplishment changed the direction of my life.

The first gift was that I gained something that my life lacked before: a dream. Having a dream to write and sell a movie literally brought passion, energy, and excitement into my life. And the beauty of a dream is that you are invigorated with each step taken toward realizing it, without having to wait for the final outcome. My dream has since evolved into helping others to recognize their own spiritual nature and to grow closer to God. I feel so driven and motivated by this passion, and I have never been so thrilled to be alive.

Second, I saw how I had come to limit my potential. I had allowed myself to get stuck in the comfortable and predictable routine of life. In writing a movie, I allowed myself to think "bigger" and strive for more.

If my movie never sells, I still win. I win from the perspective that I set out to do something challenging for me, and I did it. And it has been easy for me to extrapolate from that experience. Now I literally feel that anything I have an interest in, I can pursue. Yet the world has always been there for my taking, I just didn't permit myself to see it that way. I have learned that through striving for difficult challenges, even if I am unsuccessful, I gain, for I am now a proactive player in my life. We can be our own greatest limitation; our potential is great exactly to the extent that we choose to tap into it.

When I opened the door to my own personal potential, I also opened the door to life's potential for me. I no longer thought with boundaries. Anything and everything became possible. When my spiritual week presented itself, I was willing to cast aside my comfort with my existing relationship with God, as well as my fear of a new and different relationship with Him. I was willing to trust my heart and the possibilities presented by God.

But as I have said before, our growth with God and in our own spirituality requires our willingness and effort. We have to focus on exactly where we want to go and who we want to be and strive for it, and then focus and strive again, and then focus and strive again. Just as a baby must sit up before she crawls, and crawl before she walks, we too have steps we must follow in our spiritual growth.

But the glorious news is that we can take those steps anytime we decide to and that when we seek God's help and guidance to grow with Him, He will guide us. If we free ourselves from our limitations and expectations, God will take us to greater and more joyous, peaceful, loving places than we think possible. The amazing part is that when you reach that place beyond your imagination, you are able to see that you can go even farther.

Let go of your rock, test the waters, and renew your growth with God. For God is love, God is infinite, and God is limitless. And do you know what? So are we!

APPENDIX A

Trey's Perspective

I WAS DRIVING THROUGH THE MOUNTAINS on a beautiful Sunday afternoon recently with my older daughter. As usual, she was peppering me with questions, exercising her inquisitive mind and challenging mine. We were talking about relationships when finally she got around to asking about my views of marriage to her mother.

What I told her was this: "I have always been fortunate in everything that mattered, and marrying Jenice was no exception. Although we have had our ups and downs, we have always had a good marriage, mostly because we both cared deeply about the same things. Then, one day a few years ago, my marriage and my life went from being great to being beyond anything I could have ever imagined. I have always been thankful when praying, but now when I pray, the thing I am most thankful for is the incredible gift of getting to live an awakened life, which was given to me through your mother and her remarkable experiences."

But most people familiar with Jenice's experiences do not ask me the same questions as my daughter, who is not the least bit restrained by normal boundaries—of privacy or otherwise. Instead, those who know me, and many who don't, have asked the other questions: How did I know it was "real?" Why didn't I think Jenice was crazy? Wasn't I concerned about what we were getting into?

To answer those questions, I need to provide some sense of where I was when all of this started. Although respectful of all religions and others' views, my own view was that I knew or understood that there was a God, but I did not believe that God was active in human history. I recognized that this put me at odds with every religious text ever written, but I did not see evidence of the interaction between human beings and God in my own life, and, in fact, I saw too many instances of senseless suffering to believe that God was actively involved with our dramas on earth.

Instead, I reasoned, God gave us this precious gift of free will and then got out of the way. Although this was consistent with what I perceived about the world at the time, I still could not answer one question, despite plenty of searching, and that question was the one that seemed to be at the heart of everything: Why are we here? What is our purpose?

I had looked hard enough at this question to know that the answer that seemed to be provided by organized religions did not ring true to me, although I greatly valued the words of those religious teachers whom I found to be genuine and wise. Similarly, I had not had any experiences that I would characterize at the time as being "spiritual" in nature; I never felt "plugged in" as some others seemed to be.

I did know that Jenice was connected to something beyond ourselves, however, because of a sad but bizarre event that occurred several years prior to the experiences described in this book. Late one evening after returning from out of town, Jenice and I were settling in at home, getting ready for the week ahead, when Jenice suddenly felt very ill and went to the bathroom with dry heaves for about five minutes. Then, just as quickly as the whole thing had begun, it passed, and Jenice felt fine, as though nothing had happened.

When we found out a few hours later that Jenice's seemingly unexplainable dry heaves had occurred at exactly the same time that Craig was choking to death, I knew that Jenice had felt Craig's desperate struggle. Through the haze of unfathomable pain that defined that evening, one thing stood out for me clearly: Jenice was tapped into something beyond ourselves.

As we worked through the grief of Craig's death over the next year and beyond, I would occasionally tell Jenice how remarkable I found her physical experiencing of Craig's death, but she never seemed to be particularly impressed. (I never knew if that was because she thought it was inappropriate to focus on her own "gift" in the face of Craig's death, or because she already knew she was connected, or for some other reason.) In any event, the episode stuck in my mind as a clear indication that Jenice was connected in some way that most people are not. Later, I realized that Jenice's character as a deeply feeling person, which made it so difficult at times for her to deal with the overwhelming grief over the loss of her brother, also was the means for her connection to the spiritual realm. In other words, the flip side to having to feel pain so intensely was that she was also sensitive enough to consciously feel the contact of a loving spirit in another body or beyond the physical world.

So when the events of May 1996 began to unfold, I had some frame of reference in which to place those events. I still have to laugh about finding myself on the other side of an awakening experience. I think most people who know me, or at least who knew me then, would describe me as being logical, rational, and even-keeled. I have always loved to think analytically, and I have relied heavily on my analytical skills in my career as a corporate attorney. The analytical approach is not particularly helpful, however, when your wife comes up to you one pleasant Sunday afternoon and says, "You're not going to believe what just happened; I just saw that psychic's aura."

The truth is that I found myself in May 1996 in an area where I couldn't just use my mind to explain what was going on, because the experiences were beyond anything my mind comprehended at the time. I had to be willing to "go with the flow" with a sense of openness and trust in order to be a part of everything that unfolded. And that is exactly what I did. My mind did know some very important things, however, which I believe helped enable me to open up to an intuitive view of what was happening.

First, I knew Jenice very well. I knew that she was at a very good, content place in life when these events unfolded. She was not under any stress or seeking something to bring peace in her life. Rather, we both were at a place where we were very aware of and grateful for the many blessings that seemed to just keep coming our way. (Of course, they were just beginning.) At other times in our life together that had not been the case. I had seen Jenice as she struggled mightily to deal with the death of her brother several years before. If she had started to hear voices then, I probably would have been very unlikely to accept them as a gift from God—although I now recognize that I would probably have been wrong in making that judgment.

Second, although I never felt plugged in spiritually myself, I at least knew one other person who did—our friend Erin. I deeply respected Erin and appreciated it when she shared the stories of some of her spiritual experiences, even though they seemed foreign to me. I have always tried to respect everyone's experiences and views, but with Erin I had to do more than that. Erin was an incredibly successful venture capitalist, with a remarkable gift for analyzing business opportunities and structuring business transactions. She had no reason to undermine her credibility by talking about connecting to things outside of our normal scope of perception. I also had known her for over twenty years. I might not have understood what she was describing, but I had every reason to believe that she was telling the truth.

Finally, I had one other tremendous advantage in understanding and accepting what was unfolding, as compared to the many family members and friends whom we have shared this with: I could speak to the Guides myself. Although Amy and High Guide had to use Jenice's body to communicate, when they did, I could easily distinguish between them and Jenice. Amy was helpful and caring, with a spirit of fun and often silliness. For example, instead of saying "Exactly" as Jenice would, Amy would say "Exa-ca-la-ca-la-ca-ly," just to make herself giggle. High Guide, on the other hand, was serious and wise, like an erudite professor, which was no more like Jenice than Amy's impishness.

Still, at the early part of the week I did have my doubts. This was the great unknown, and the well-being of the person I cared most about was at stake. So I did the only thing I could think of: I prayed. I prayed for protection for Jenice, and I prayed for a sense of peace and understanding for me so that I could know what was right. After that I could only go with my intuition, which was that Jenice should trust her intuition and go along with these bizarre developments until it no longer felt right for her to do so. In the meantime, we would discuss everything, turning it over in our minds, trying to understand what it all meant and where it all was going.

The week itself was almost surreal. I was in a ridiculously busy stage at work, coming home very late and then working at home even later yet. Even so, Jenice and I would still talk for at least an hour each evening. Instead of feeling worn down by the grueling pace at the office coupled with the consistent late night discussions, I felt very energized, as did Jenice. With hindsight, it was as if we both could feel the magnitude of what was coming, even if we did not know what it was. It was very exciting.

Even so, the week was not without its moments of doubt for both of us. The most troubling part for me was that I found myself aroused (physically) on a couple of occasions as Jenice would meditate and try to make those initial connections with her guides. Although I do not feel particularly burdened by any of the hang-ups about sex that our culture generates in seemingly limitless quantities, I still was very uncomfortable with the thought that I was going along with all of this because of some base physical interest rather than what seemed to be our highest good. Still, I could not tell that this was not for our highest good, so I prayed and kept going with the flow.

Then, as the contact began and the messages came through, I had no doubt that this was a wonderful, incredible gift. The first moment when that became clear to me was early Friday morning on May 10th. Although we had slept very little throughout the week and although Jenice has never been an early riser, she woke me up around 5:00 a.m. and began to describe her new understanding of herself, myself, and our relationship together.

Prior to that morning, I had always prided myself on being the one who was willing to address our issues more directly. I felt that I was more often the one who would push the conversation so that the anger, frustration, disappointment, or other emotion that was being expressed would not be the last form of communication between us on an issue. I also felt that this approach may have been painful for us at times but that it had truly helped our relationship. Still, I knew there were parts of Jenice that I didn't really expect to ever be able to reach, and I knew that I had barriers of my own that I was unlikely to abandon for fear of what might be left if I did.

And so, early on that Friday morning, I found myself listening to my wife describing our issues in a way that was so clear and so accurate, and at the same time so loving and nonjudgmental, that I sat there quietly and let the tears roll down my face. Before that morning, I knew we could love each other and help each other through hardship. I knew we could be good parents. I knew we could, in humble ways, make a difference in the lives of others. But before that morning I never knew that I could have a marriage in which our worst fears, our most guarded unspeakables, could be gently and lovingly thrust into the light so that there was a very real possibility that they could be dismantled and a deeper, stronger love could be born.

That is what I meant when I told my daughter that my marriage went from being great to being beyond anything I could have ever imagined. I knew Jenice's boundaries as well as the limitations that I had imposed, and I never dreamed that we could actually sweep them all away. I was willing to stay committed for a lifetime and I was content to put in the effort whenever needed to have a beautiful relationship—and then I got a glimpse of what a beautiful relationship was!

When Jenice called me later in the morning to tell me about her Jesus encounter, it seemed like a glorious culmination of what had already been a miraculous day and week. For the first time in our relationship, I began to experience the same sensations as Jenice that day. Just as Jenice felt like she was in a fog, finding it very difficult to concentrate, I struggled with focusing on my activities throughout the day. I was particularly challenged when I had to chair a meeting during the lunch hour, even though that normally would have been an easy task. When Jenice later described her difficulty in handling even some of the simplest interactions during the day, I knew that we were starting to be connected to each other in a way we had not been before.

In the few days that followed, Jenice was at a truly remarkable place. She had an uncanny insight into our children and their issues, which she described as seeing them through "spiritual eyes." As with her comments about our relationship, her insights into our children were accurate and loving and addressed the essence of the matter. There was no element of frustration or anxiety as there might have been in the past.

She was equally incredible with the unruly rabble of third-graders that we called our Sunday School class. Where normally we struggled to maintain even a modicum of control over this good but often difficult bunch, Jenice held their rapt attention the entire class. As with our own children, they could feel the difference in her and they were drawn to her. Jenice in turn shared beautiful insights and her pervading sense of peace and calm, which they seemed to genuinely appreciate.

After the unparalleled beauty of May 10, I did not have any doubts. In fact, independent of Jenice I made a conscious choice that day to "give my will to God." I was driving down the highway to my lunch meeting, reflecting on the events of the morning, when I realized that I had reached a fork in the path. We had received so much help to get to this incredible day. High Guide, Amy, and now Jesus were assisting us directly. Paradoxically it was incredibly humbling and gratifying at the same time. It was also as if the spirit world (as I conceived it then) were opening a door and asking if we would go through it. I said yes.

Over the months and now years since May 1996, so many beautiful things have happened. For one, the wisdom shared by Jenice's guides has been confirmed many times over in our readings and in our experience. It also seemed so simple and so intuitively right. Our guides were not trying to get us to do anything, they were only teaching us that our entire earthly existence is about bringing more love into ourselves and the world around us. We each are children of God, incredibly valued, incredibly loved. And we each will experience the very things that our souls need most in order to help us on our path.

At first it seemed almost too good to be true. We are here to experience ourselves on a journey of becoming greater and greater love. We are given so much more assistance than we ever realize. We have capacity to live peacefully, love fully, eat healthily, speak truthfully; we just choose otherwise. That doesn't change the truth though—we are from God, we are actually a part of God, all of us. (Would you lie to God, disrespect God? If not, then why would you lie to or disrespect another—or even worse, and just as common, lie to or disrespect yourself?) Even our own negative choices are not a cause for despair, however, as there is only one outcome for all of us in the end, and we will have all the help we need to get there.

    I now have my own sense of connection to All That Is. Even as I remain incredibly grateful for the gift of learning and growing through my conversations with Jenice's guides, I also have the comfort of truly accepting what I am—a child of God with my own gifts and my own connection to everything else. My greatest hope is that people everywhere can begin to have this same understanding in their hearts, because, as I described to my daughter, it is the greatest gift imaginable.

APPENDIX B

Channeling

A FEW FRIENDS HAVE ASKED THAT I address channeling in greater detail, and I am happy to share my experience with it. However, I feel that my perspective is rather limited, as I have not studied channeling in depth. I've only done it with Trey and not on a consistent basis, and I do not have any friends who channel, so I have no sense whether my technique is normal or off the curve. I just do it and it works, I assume because Jesus led me to this connection.

I have a couple of thoughts I'd like to share before proceeding. First, channeling is not the focus of my experience or of this book. Channeling is nothing more than a tool that was given to me to help me learn God's messages so that I can both apply them in my life and relay them to others. Although important in my spirituality, I feel that channeling is not an essential element of spirituality in general.

Second, shortly after my experience, I heard in two separate conversations within a twenty-four-hour period that channeling is not for everyone and can be potentially dangerous. Personally, I do not relate to this message, as my channeling experiences have felt completely safe and comfortable. Yet this "not coincidental" coincidence of hearing virtually identical messages within a day's time has prompted me to think further about the possible danger.

We know that not all spirits choose God's love and light. The book *Opening to Channel* advises channels to first always ask the spirit present whether it is from the light, because even spirits that are not from the light cannot lie on this matter. Channels can also trust their feelings while in the presence of a spirit. A spirit from God's love and light will never make you feel uncomfortable, guilty, or bad in any way. The book strongly suggests never to interact or communicate with the "dark" spirits out of curiosity or for any other reason. If you find yourself with one of those spirits, you should immediately tell that spirit to leave and then ask for a spirit from the light.

When I channel, I know that I am protected and at no risk of harm or abuse. Since Jesus brought my guides and me together, I know their essence and their purpose in communicating with me. Someone who channels, who has not been "assigned" guides as I have, opens up to unknown places and unknown spirits, creating a potentially dangerous situation. Yet channeling can be safe and immensely enlightening when done by a responsible and cautious person who relies on his or her sense of good versus evil and does not empower the evil. The channel always has control and can protect himself or herself. The danger is minimized, if not eliminated, when channeling is engaged for good and godly purposes, that is, from and out of love. Having said that, please understand that I am neither recommending channeling nor advising against it.

For me, meditation and channeling are closely related in that both require that I go within myself and both are enriched when I proceed without any expectations. They are different, however, in that with meditation, I free my mind and let transpire what will, and with channeling, Trey and I direct the focus by bringing up topics that we want to discuss with my guides.

With both meditation and channeling, I proceed at a time when I'm sure there will be no interruptions. I sit in a chair or on the couch with my back and head straight and upright and my feet touching the floor. My arms and hands rest either on the seat beside me or on my legs. The position of my body affects the flow of spiritual energy and thus my state of connectedness. My goal is to have a straight and upright line from my tailbone to the crown of my head. In this position, the energy has maximum, uninterrupted flow through the seven chakras or energy points aligned in the torso, neck, and head. Sitting correctly and with my eyes closed, I then relax and breathe slowly and deeply, focusing on my breathing to pull my mind away from the external environment and into myself.

With meditation, I continue on one of two courses until I am aware that I have reached my inner space. One course is to continue the focus on my breathing, and the other is to pray about whatever it is I want and need to pray about. When I'm in my inner space, I sense that I am in this large area that has boundaries to it like a room. This room feels defined by space itself, not by hard or solid walls. My inner space is warm, dark, peaceful, and comforting, and while there, I have no sense of the physical elements surrounding me, such as my body, the chair, or my house. I have withdrawn into my spirit, shedding my physicality. My thoughts transition into this loud voice, as if I'm talking in a canyon where there is no other place for them to go. Then I just let my mind go where it will. Sometimes my thoughts are enlightened, and other times my mind just enjoys the peaceful rest and seclusion of this space.

I also have a routine for coming out of meditation. I have found that when I rush to get out of my relaxed state, I am often left with a headache. So I've learned to focus on my breathing again so that I become aware of my body again. After a short while, I then move a finger or toe to bring me further into the physical. When I'm fully aware of my body and my surroundings, I open my eyes.

I've just realized that focusing on my breathing works in what would appear to be contradictory ways. When beginning to meditate, my breathing helps me to withdraw from the physical. Yet when concluding my meditation, my breathing helps me to return to the physical.

Channeling begins in the same position and with the same initial focus on breathing. The step I take that leads me down the channeling path instead of the meditation path is that I call on High Guide. With my thoughts, I first tell High Guide that I am coming to him, and then I ask for his help in connecting us. I'll share with you what I sense happens, even though it may sound odd. Immediately upon calling on High Guide, I sense a spotlight beaming out from the top of my head into the spiritual realm. It's like a phone call to High Guide. He immediately spots my light, which is distinct from any other's, and then he's with me and guides me. What I mean by guiding is that he gives me a sense of the steps I need to take to strengthen our connection so that he can use my body to talk to Trey. Although I am giving control of my body to High Guide, I can stop or refuse to follow his direction at any time.

The first thing I notice is that my breathing changes, as if the intent is to get every bit of air out of my lungs during the exhalation. This continues for several breaths, with the time between breaths lengthening. Then I reach a point where I empty all my air and I don't take another breath for several seconds. I have a bodily urge to take a breath, but I know that I shouldn't. I sense that this is when High Guide enters. When my breathing begins again, I feel that High Guide is in control of it. His breathing is rhythmic but different from my own, sometimes slower and deeper and other times faster and shallower.

Next, I focus on removing my mind from my body so that my mind won't control or limit High Guide's communication. When I first started channeling, I knew that I needed to get my mind out of High

Guide's way, but I didn't understand exactly how to do this. So I tried to move my mind over to the side, in effect, making space for High Guide. Although we were able to channel, I would often block High Guide's messages.

Trey and I both wanted as open and pure a connection with High Guide as possible, so I did some research. I learned that we each possess, as part of our being, an energy field that extends a few inches outside of our body. I liken this field to the earth's atmosphere, which is still part of the earth but not visible to the eye. With this knowledge, I am now able to remove my mind from my physical body. I visualize opening a hatch at the top of my head. I then direct my mind to pour out of my body and into the energy space surrounding my body. As you might imagine, before I was aware of our own "atmosphere," I would not have considered removing my mind from my body to let it float freely around!

When my skin warms up and I feel hot, I know that I have successfully moved my mind into my outer energy field. With my mind relocated, High Guide's and my connection transitions from my *feeling* his direction and cues to my *hearing* him. I'll hear High Guide's voice saying "Hello" softly in my head, and as our connection grows, his voice strengthens and we can carry on a conversation. Over the course of a few minutes, I feel my body progressively lighten, and eventually I feel as if it actually lifts a bit. Instead of feeling myself sitting on the couch and being pulled down by gravity, it feels as if there is a gravitational pull from above, causing my body to gently rest on the surface of the couch. Upon experiencing this lift, I know that High Guide and I are close to channeling. Sometimes it feels as if my body, particularly my hands, melts away, and other times it feels as if my body is a rigid shell that I am no longer a part of.

High Guide and I always have a short initial conversation in my head before he begins to talk to Trey. Other than an occasional "pep talk" by High Guide, these conversations are directed by me, and I use them to gain confidence in our connection. Starting the actual channeling is always a little difficult for me. The urge is to talk like I normally talk—I have a thought, then I speak it—but I can no longer orally communicate my thoughts. My mouth literally will not move when I have something to say. It is a really bizarre feeling. To help me first release the natural tendency to speak myself and then give control of my vocal cords and mouth to High Guide, I go through this little ritual of asking High Guide to specifically say, "Hello, Trey." Once I have let High Guide say those words, I no longer try to control my mouth.

Our connection is weakest at the beginning of the session and grows stronger as Trey and High Guide converse. High Guide's voice, which is my voice, starts off monotone and faint, with his sentences often spoken in pieces. It is similar to the fragmented speech of a person on a respirator who gets part of a thought out and then takes a breath and gets more of the thought out. As the session continues and the connection strengthens, so does the flow of the conversation as well as the strength of High Guide's voice.

My connection with High Guide varies from time to time depending on my moods. If I am stressed or impatient because of a difficult day, then our connection is usually weaker. During our most strongly connected sessions, I take on High Guide's energy. From my perspective, High Guide's voice turns masculine, and I actually sense his shape around my body. My hands and arms and chest seem to grow larger, and even though my eyes are closed, I feel as though I am peering out of High Guide's face, like there is a mask of a man's face covering my own. One of these times Trey was actually able to see High Guide, or the energy of High Guide, around me.

During Trey and High Guide's conversations, I'm talked about in the third person. When I want to tell Trey something, I tell High Guide to relay the message. High Guide often keeps Trey informed of how I'm feeling or reacting to their conversation. High Guide typically does not have an agenda and lets Trey choose the topics of conversation, although he has on a few occasions led us to discussions we didn't anticipate. On one such occasion, I was able to detach myself enough from my body so that I could actually feel Trey's emotions. With High Guide's assistance, I stepped into Trey's shoes, that is, his energy. It was amazing.

Our channeling is like counseling sessions. When we go to High Guide, he doesn't just rattle off God's truths. Instead, Trey (and I) addresses issues we're working on, insights we're starting to see, the purpose behind events in our lives, and everything else that is helpful for us to grow with love and with God. High Guide listens, discusses, and helps us to understand the workings of God more clearly; that is, he *guides* us to the truth.

When our channeling session is over, I am always physically exhausted. Trey and I will usually discuss certain parts of the conversation that we found particularly interesting or that Trey wasn't completely clear on. While Trey hears only the words themselves, I grasp the truth of the message and I understand the context and the dynamic of the topic, I assume because I am in a heightened spiritual state during channeling. We usually channel after the kids have gone to bed, for obvious reasons, so after our review I typically head straight for bed for a very peaceful night's sleep.

Channeling is very similar to dreaming for me. When the session first ends, I can remember everything discussed, yet with time the specifics of the discussion fade. So Trey tends to remember the specifics of the conversations, and I tend to retain the bigger-picture understanding. We try to tape-record our sessions or at least make notes after the session is over, in case over time our memories fail us.

Channeling takes many different forms. I see myself as having channeled in three different ways, all of which have been conscious channeling. The channeling I have described in this chapter is oral channeling, with High Guide using my body to speak to Trey. Then there is mental channeling as I was able to do with High Guide and

Amy while I was still at a higher spiritual realm after my spiritual week. We just conversed in my head without my needing to meditate or get into a "trance." I'm guessing that mental channeling is what legitimate psychics do. And finally I have channeled through writing. During my spiritual week and for a time afterwards, Amy used my arm and hand to write me messages.

Just as different forms of channeling exist, the way the channel receives information varies also. According to *Opening to Channel*:

> In conscious channeling the guide impresses the message upon your mind through what might be called higher telepathy. . . . Some people "know" the message (called clairsentient), some "see" the information (clairvoyant), and some people "hear" the information (clairaudient). Some receive the transmission as a richness of impressions that they then match with words.

Typically, I feel that I am a clairsentient, although at times I feel as if I receive impressions that I then match with words.

I thought that I might touch on psychics a little further, although I have to qualify this discussion because I'm not acquainted with any psychic nor have I talked to one about my theory. Additionally, as with channeling, I am neither recommending nor advising against the use of a psychic. Personally, I tend to seek a psychic only on rare occasions, maybe when I'm stuck on an issue or would like confirmation, as I now know that I possess, as do you, the ability to discover my own answers by turning within myself.

I understand the entertainment value of talking to a psychic. If that is your purpose, then play the game as you wish and have fun with it. But I now view psychics from a more serious and credible perspective because of my experience with channeling. I believe that psychics are able to tap into the spiritual realm and receive messages from spiritual guides. I used to think, as many of us probably do, that psychics read both our minds and the future. That is an incorrect assumption that causes us to look to the psychic for specific facts about ourselves in order for them to have credibility. If the psychic can tell you things such as your name, how old you are, what you do for a living, or how many children you have, then you are more likely to believe him or her. That focus, however, gets us off course because that is not the guide's purpose. The purpose of guides is to help us in our spiritual growth and evolution, not to recount meaningless facts to prove their existence. They accomplish their purpose by helping us to see the true dynamic of our lives and where our decisions are leading us. In this regard, they are giving us the most likely outcome of our futures. This is not predicting the future, as the future is not set. Through free will, we have control to change our lives and who we are with every decision we make.

So if you truly want guidance, it is important that you give the guide, through the psychic, all of the relevant information on the topic you wish to address. With the most direct, honest, and complete information from you, the guide can give you the most accurate and insightful advice. This makes sense when you think about it. The guide is working through the psychic's energy, not through yours, except to the extent that you open up to him or her.

Psychics are effectively translators, which allows for human error to occur. A good psychic will just relay the information received without interpreting it or putting it into a specific context. In fact, the psychic may not understand the answer or even the question. What you do with the information conveyed is also important. Our tendency is to apply the message to something in our lives rather than to let the meaning unfold. I prematurely applied the psychic's messages on the day my spiritual experience began, by putting them into the context of my screenwriting, and I was even able to lead the psychic into the same assumptions. Over time I discovered that the psychic's messages had broader, deeper meanings that I now more fully understand.

Whether with channeling or psychic readings, it is important for both the person receiving the reading and the channel or psychic relaying the information to avoid placing their own expectations or interpretations on the messages received. If we avoid literal interpretations and instead just openly receive what the spiritual realm offers, we free ourselves to be guided down more meaningful paths.

Closing Thoughts

WHATEVER DOUBTS, INSECURITIES, UNCERTAINTIES that I initially felt about sharing my experience with others are now gone. I fully rejoice in the opportunity to be a messenger of God's love, light, and truth. My experiences shared in this book were just the beginning of my experience of God. My connection with the Divine continues to grow and evolve and is significantly richer and broader than I ever imagined possible. I am blessed; I am grateful from the depth of my soul. I am love. I am God's.

Throughout Part II of this book, I interchanged the masculine and feminine pronoun for God. My intent was to broaden our perspective of God from the Christian imagery of the bearded grandfather watching over us from Heaven to an understanding that God is so much more. I hope that every time I wrote "She" some will stop for a moment to rethink their conceptualization of God. God is not a person, although Jesus is God personified, and for that matter, so are we. Rather, God is energy, creation manifesting, formless yet everything. I recognize that my approach is flawed as "She" still implies that God is a person, but at least it captures the feminine essence or qualities of God, in addition to the masculine ones. I long for the ability to describe the indescribable, and yet I believe that it is our experience of God that allows us to understand that which is beyond words.

Although I wrote *Diary of an Awakening*, I have released it to God. It is not mine—it is God's. I always know that the message is not about me or by me, but through me. Early in the writing process, my guides gave me a beautiful image of this book. They said to imagine it as a kite with each of my personal, earthly expectations represented as a string attached to it. Until I cut the strings by releasing my concerns, the kite could not fly to reach its highest potential. I have willingly, and gratefully, severed my ego-based ties to allow God to reach others through *Diary of an Awakening* in His way, to let it soar with the gentle breeze of His breath. I thank you for sharing with me, and I pray for your growth with God, for your journey to truth and greater love.

God's love,

Jenice Cutler

If you would like to contact Jenice or receive a free *Diary of an Awakening* Readers Guide, then please visit:

www.inneravenue.com

Jenice Meagher Cutler, a former business attorney, is a writer and stay-at-home mother. Although Texans for thirty-six years, Jenice and her husband, Trey, now live in Colorado with their three children.